To Jeffry

With Love

Aunt Muriam

and

Uncle Jack

EXPLORING SPACE

DERRYDALE BOOKS
New York

Some material copyright© MCMLXXVII by Grolier Ltd.
Some material copyright© MCMLXXIV by Waverly House Ltd.
Some material copyright© MCMLXXIX by Banner Press, Inc.

This edition is published by Derrydale Books,
a division of Crown Publishers, Inc.,
by arrangement with Banner Press, Inc.
a   b   c   d   e   f   g   h

DERRYDALE 1979 EDITION

Manufactured in the United States of America

Library of Congress Cataloging in Publication Data
Exploring space.
    SUMMARY: Text and pictures introduce the story of
man in space, past, present, and future.
    1. Astronautics—Juvenile literature.
[1. Astronautics] I.   Gonzalez, Linda Timko.
TL793.E96   629.4   79-53951
ISBN 0-517-29545-8

CONTENTS

Stars and Constellations

If you look up into a clear night sky, you will see about 3,000 twinkling points of light. Among these may be Mercury, Venus, Mars, Jupiter and Saturn. Like the earth, these planets are shining with the sun's reflected light. But the other twinkling points of light are stars. These large bodies of gas produce their own energy and send out their own light. Our own sun is a star. It is 1,300,000 times the size of the earth. But, as stars go, it is tiny.

The stars stretch out across the universe as far as our most powerful telescopes can see. They are arranged in huge islands of stars called galaxies. Our sun and its planets lie within one of these galaxies— the Milky Way. This appears as a wide milk-colored band of light stretching across the night sky.

At the beginning of the 17th century, Galileo, the Italian scientist, turned his telescope to the Milky Way. He soon discovered that its cloud-like band of light was made up of uncountable pin-

A million stars surround the Veil nebula in the constellation Cygnus.

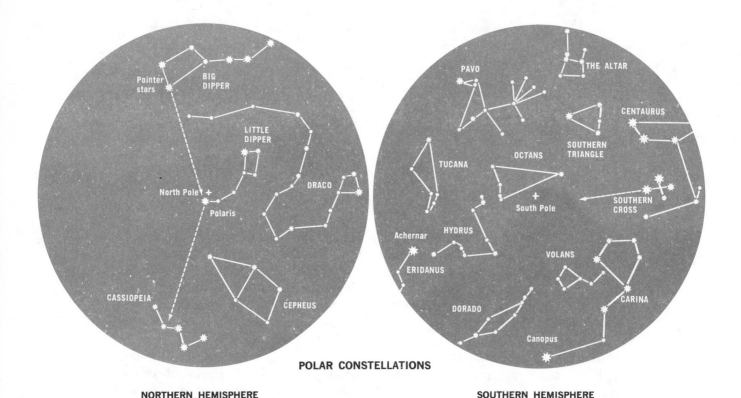

POLAR CONSTELLATIONS

NORTHERN HEMISPHERE   SOUTHERN HEMISPHERE

points of light—each one a star. Scientists now estimate that the Milky Way contains about 150,000,000,000 stars.

Distances between the galaxies—and between the stars that lie in the same galaxy—are vast. In fact, they are so vast that they are measured in *light-years*, not miles or kilometers. One light-year is the distance that light travels in one year—almost 6,000,000,000,000 miles (9,656,000,000,000 kilometers). Through its center, the Milky Way is about 20,000 light-years thick, and is about 100,000 light-years long. The closest star that we can see without a telescope—Alpha Centauri—is just over 4 light-years away.

PATTERNS OF STARS

The word 'galaxy' comes from a Greek word meaning 'milky'. The ancient Greeks applied it to the only galaxy they knew of—our own Milky Way. This they simply called 'the Galaxy'. Even today, when many other galaxies have been discovered, 'the Galaxy' always means our own.

Astronomers of ancient Egypt, Greece and other lands discovered that many of the stars they could see in the Milky Way were arranged in certain interesting patterns, or *constellations*. Around the 5th century B.C. the Greeks began to give names to these star patterns. Many of the names they chose came from the rich store of Greek myths—especially the fabulous voyage of the Argonauts.

A few centuries later, the Romans translated these names into their own Latin language. And it is by their Latin names that many of the constellations are known today. Modern astronomers have mapped out the constellations on map charts—each chart covering a certain section of the sky.

Signs of the Zodiac

There are 88 constellations, each one commonly known by its Latin name. Of

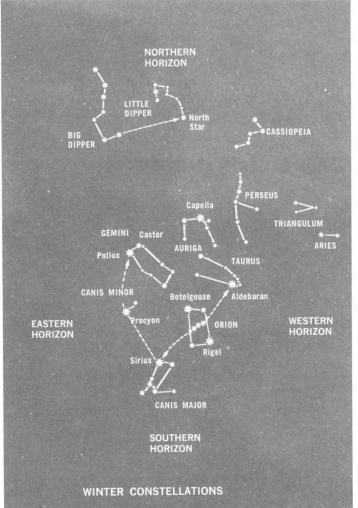

WINTER CONSTELLATIONS

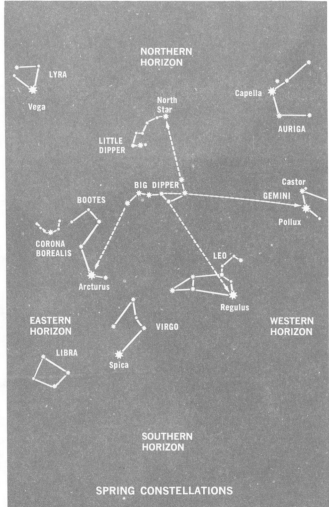

SPRING CONSTELLATIONS

these 88, 12 constellations are of particular interest to many people. These people—followers of *astrology*—believe that the 12 'signs of the Zodiac' have the power to affect events on earth. By studying their position in the night sky, astrologers believe they can tell what will happen in the future.

Each person on earth, astrologers believe, was born under one or other of these 12 constellations; which one depends on the person's date of birth. The Latin names of these constellations (with the English names in brackets) are: Aries (the Ram), Taurus (the Bull), Gemini (the Twins), Cancer (the Crab), Leo (the Lion), Virgo (the Virgin), Libra (the Scales), Scorpio (the Scorpion),

Sagittarius (the Archer), Capricorn (the Goat), Aquarius (the Water-Carrier) and Pisces (the Two Fish).

Other well-known constellations are Orion (the Hunter), Andromeda (the Chained Lady), Ursa Major (the Great Bear, better known as the Plough) and Cygnus (the Swan).

WHAT ARE STARS LIKE?

No two stars are the same. They differ in size, brightness and color. Some are hotter than others. With modern instruments scientists can measure these differences with great accuracy. From their measurements they can work out a great deal about the stars and their behavior.

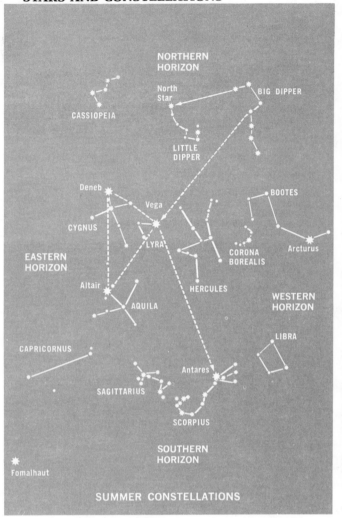

SUMMER CONSTELLATIONS

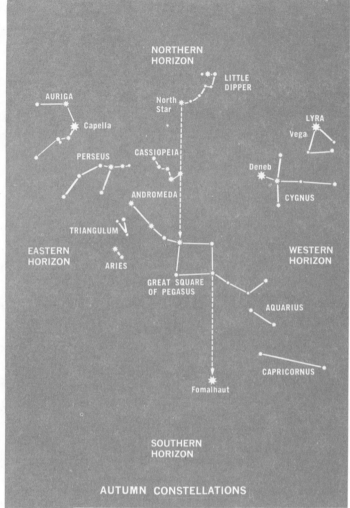

AUTUMN CONSTELLATIONS

Bright or Dim

The brightness of a star is called its *magnitude*. The astronomers of ancient Greece were the first to introduce a scale of magnitude for the stars. They thought that the brightness of a star depended on its size. That is why they used magnitude to measure brightness. ('Magnitude' means 'size'.) On the Greek scale, the brightest stars were of the first magnitude. The faintest stars were of the sixth magnitude.

Today astronomers use a scale somewhat similar to that of the Greeks. On this scale the faintest stars that can be seen without telescopes are of the sixth magnitude. Stars that are two and a half times brighter belong to the fifth mag-

nitude. Stars that are two and a half times brighter than this are of the fourth magnitude. The scale continues to zero and into the negative numbers (-1, -2, and so on). The brightest objects in the sky have a negative magnitude. Sirius, the brightest star that can be seen with the unaided eye (except for the sun) has a magnitude of -1.4. The sun has a magnitude of -27.

Astronomers know that the brightness of a star in the sky does not depend only on the star's size. Some stars look brighter than others because they are closer to the earth. If Sirius and the more distant Pollux (whose magnitude is $+1.1$) were the same distance from the earth, Pollux would be brighter.

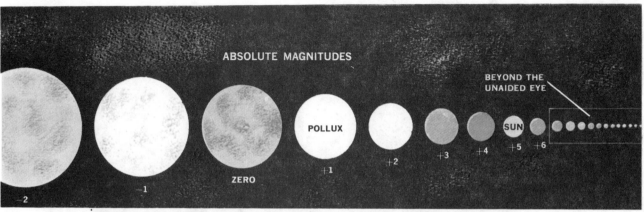

ABSOLUTE MAGNITUDES

BEYOND THE
UNAIDED EYE

POLLUX

ZERO

+1

+2

+3

+4

SUN

+5

+6

−1

−2

The very brightest stars have negative magnitudes. Originally, all bright stars were given a magnitude of 1. But better measurements showed that some first-magnitude stars were much brighter than others. The scale was then extended to negative numbers.

Thus, there are two different ways to describe the brightness of a star. One way is to describe how bright the star seems to us on earth. This is called its *apparent magnitude*. The other way is to describe how bright it really is. This is the star's *absolute magnitude*.

To measure absolute magnitude, astronomers imagine that all stars are the same distance from the earth. They agree on a distance of about 32·6 light-years. The absolute magnitude of any star is the amount of brightness a star would have if it were 32·6 light-years away from earth. For example, the sun has a very high apparent magnitude because it is close to earth. But if the sun were 32·6 light-years away, it would be a faint, fifth-magnitude star.

Hot or Cold

The brightest stars—those with the greatest absolute magnitudes—are thousands of times brighter than the sun. They are also bigger than the sun and are usually very hot. Some of the brightest stars have surface temperatures of about 36,000° C (64,832° F) or higher. Deneb, a hot star in the constellation Cygnus, is almost 5,000 times brighter than the sun. Rigel, a very hot blue star in the constellation Orion, is 21,000 times brighter than the sun.

The dimmest stars—those with the smallest absolute magnitudes—are thousands of times dimmer than the sun. Dim stars are usually small. Usually they are fairly cool, with surface temperatures of about 3,000° C (5,432° F). Dim, cool stars are small as stars go—perhaps only a tenth the size of our sun and containing one hundredth of its matter. Such stars can only be seen through telescopes.

Red, White and Blue Stars

Scientists have used sensitive instruments to test the colors of stars. They may all look the same color to the naked eye, but there are no two stars of exactly the same color. Each star sends out one color more strongly than the others.

A star's color depends on how hot the star is. Very hot stars, such as Alnilam, are blue. The cooler Sirius is bluish white. The sun, cooler still, shines with a yellow light. The coolest stars of all are red or orange.

Scientists have found that very bright

large stars are usually very hot and shine with a bluish color. Smaller, dimmer stars are usually cooler; they may be yellowish or orange, depending on their temperature. The dimmest and smallest stars of all are usually also the coolest and have an orange or reddish color.

GIANT AND DWARF STARS

No two stars are the same size. The universe contains stars that are many millions of times larger than our sun, and others that are smaller than the earth. The large stars are called giants or —the largest of all—supergiants. Yet many of these huge, bright stars are cool and reddish. Aldebaran, in the constellation Taurus, is a red giant. It is more than 50,000 times larger than the sun. Betelgeuse, in the constellation Orion,

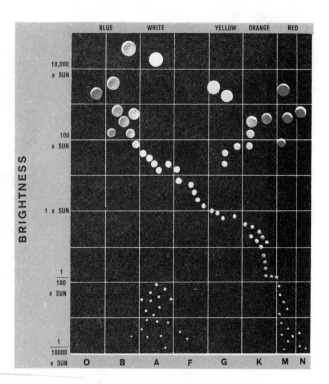

This special astronomy chart divides the stars into eight main groups. Those shown here are categorized according to their color and brightness.

Sirius, the closer star, appears brighter than Pollux. Sirius has a greater apparent magnitude than Pollux. But if the two stars were the same distance from earth, Pollux would be brighter. Pollux has a greater absolute magnitude than Sirius.

is a red supergiant more than 30,000,000 times larger than the sun.

There are also blue and blue-white giants and supergiants. For example, Rigel, in the constellation Orion, is a blue-white supergiant. All these giant stars are much larger than ordinary stars of the same color. This is because gases in a giant star are spread much more thinly than the gases in an ordinary star, such as the sun.

Some stars are very small. Because these stars are hot and white, they should be large and bright. Instead, they are small and dim. Such stars are called white dwarfs because they are much smaller than the ordinary white stars. There are also yellowish, orange or red dwarf stars.

Dwarf stars are very small. Some are only about an eighth the size of the earth.

A white dwarf may contain as much matter as the sun, but this matter is packed into a much smaller volume. The matter is packed so tightly that a piece of a white dwarf no larger than a marble would weigh a ton or more on the earth.

STARS THAT KEEP CHANGING

Most stars shine continuously with the same brightness. But there are some stars that change in brightness. They are called *variable* stars.

Red giants are often variable stars. Some of them grow brighter slowly and steadily, and then slowly and steadily grow dimmer again. Mira, in the constellation Cetus, is such a star. It takes a little less than a year for Mira to grow bright, then dim, and then bright again.

Other variables are less regular in the way their brightness changes. They remain at a steady brightness for several years, suddenly grow brighter and then return to their original brightness. The change in brightness is not very large. Such variable stars are called irregular variables. Betelgeuse is a star of this kind.

Another kind of variable star is the Cepheid variable. (The most noticeable variable star of this kind is Delta, in the constellation Cepheus; hence the name.) The Cepheid variables grow brighter and dimmer very quickly, within weeks or even a few days. Polaris, the North Star, is a Cepheid variable, but its changes in brightness are too small to be observed easily.

Scientists do not fully understand what happens when a star changes in brightness. They think that the variable stars are pulsating—that is, the stars are expanding and shrinking. And while they pulsate, their brightness—and temperature, too—constantly changes.

Exploding Stars

On rare occasions astronomers have discovered what seem to be new stars.

Two stages in the life of a supernova. Above: August 1937—supernova at its greatest brightness. Below: November 1938—film exposed twice as long as one above reveals only a faint dot where the brilliant star once shone.

In fact these stars had existed before their discovery but were too dim to be seen. Why, then, do the stars suddenly become bright enough to be seen? Astronomers believe that these stars are exploding. When a star explodes, it becomes so bright that it is suddenly noticed by astronomers, just as if it were a new star coming into being. Because the star appears to be new, it is called a *nova*. (*Nova* is the Latin word for 'new'.) A nova usually grows thousands of times brighter in about two days, then slowly fades. In these two days, the nova may send out more energy—light and heat—than our sun does in 30,000 years.

Sometimes, but very rarely, a star explodes with even greater force than a nova. It grows millions of times brighter than it had been before. Then it is called a supernova. The remains of a supernova that exploded in 1054 can be seen today in the constellation Taurus. It is called the Crab nebula.

Astronomers think a star becomes a nova or supernova when nuclear reactions inside the star build up energy faster than the star can emit it (give it out). The result is an explosion. The star is not destroyed, but an outer layer of gases is blown out into space. The star may undergo this process several times in its life.

Twinkling Twins

Some stars change in brightness because they are *binary* stars. A binary star is made up of two stars that are orbiting each other. Sometimes the two stars are like each other, but they may be very different. Sirius, for example, is a binary made up of a bluish-white star somewhat larger than the sun and a much smaller white dwarf.

Not all binaries change in brightness.

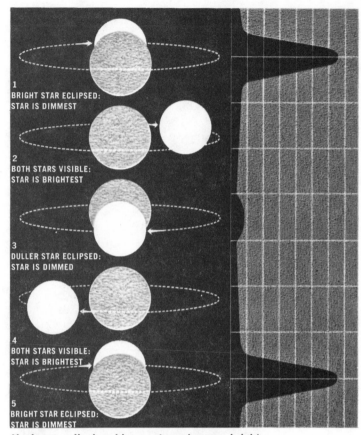

1 BRIGHT STAR ECLIPSED: STAR IS DIMMEST

2 BOTH STARS VISIBLE: STAR IS BRIGHTEST

3 DULLER STAR ECLIPSED: STAR IS DIMMED

4 BOTH STARS VISIBLE: STAR IS BRIGHTEST

5 BRIGHT STAR ECLIPSED: STAR IS DIMMEST

Algol—an eclipsing binary star—changes brightness as one star is eclipsed by the other. The diagram shows different positions of the stars: the graph shows the changing pattern of brightness.

Such a change happens only if one of the stars in the binary crosses in front of the other star and, as seen from the earth, eclipses it. In some binary stars, one star may be totally eclipsed by the other, so that the light of only one star is seen. This kind of binary is called an *eclipsing binary*. Algol, in the constellation Perseus, is an eclipsing binary.

Some of the points of light you see in the sky are made up of several stars. Castor, in the constellation of Gemini, is made up of six stars—three binary systems orbiting one another. Stars like Castor are called multiple stars.

HOW A STAR IS FORMED

A new star is formed when pressure and temperature inside the whirling ball of gases are so high that nuclear reactions begin to take place.

Seen from opposite ends of earth's orbit, a nearby star seems to change position with relation to more distant stars. The nearby star's parallax is half this angle of shift. A star's parallax is used in calculating distance of star from sun.

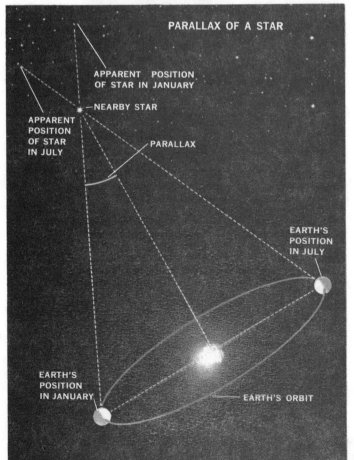

PARALLAX OF A STAR

APPARENT POSITION OF STAR IN JANUARY

NEARBY STAR

APPARENT POSITION OF STAR IN JULY

PARALLAX

EARTH'S POSITION IN JULY

EARTH'S POSITION IN JANUARY

EARTH'S ORBIT

A STAR IS BORN—AND DIES

Stars do not shine forever. They come into existence, shine for millions or billions of years, and then stop shining.

Stars come into existence in the vast clouds of dust and gas that move through space. A star begins to form when a large number of gas particles join together within such a cloud. The gravitational pull of the whirling particles attracts more particles. As the group of particles slowly gets larger and larger, its gravitational pull gets stronger and stronger. The particles draw in towards one another and form a giant ball of gas.

As the number of gas particles in the ball grows larger, the particles press down on those below them and pressure builds up inside the ball. Finally the pressure becomes strong enough to raise the temperature of the gases and the ball of gases begins to glow. When the pressure and temperature inside the ball get very high, nuclear reactions begin to take place. The gases have become a star. This process of star formation probably takes a few million years.

If a large amount of matter comes together in forming a star, the star will be large, bright and hot. Because it is hot, the star will burn up its nuclear fuel in about 100,000,000 years. If the star is made up of much smaller amounts of matter, it will be small, dim and cool. It will burn up its fuel slowly and may shine for thousands of millions of years.

A Star's Energy

Stars contain a great deal of hydrogen, which is their main source of energy. Stars also contain many different chemical elements, such as helium, nitrogen, oxygen, iron, nickel and zinc. All these elements are in the form of gases.

Stars emit large amounts of heat and

15

light and other forms of energy. The amount of energy a star emits depends on the size of the star and on the kind of star it is.

Scientists have learned that a star gets its energy from reactions that take place deep within the star. These reactions are not chemical reactions, like the burning of coal or wood. They are nuclear reactions—reactions that take place between the nuclei, or center parts, of atoms.

The nuclear reactions in the stars are like the nuclear reactions that take place when a hydrogen bomb explodes. During the reactions, the nuclei of hydrogen atoms come together. The hydrogen nuclei combine and form helium nuclei. Some of the mass of the nuclei changes into energy—heat, light and other kinds of energy. A very small amount of matter can produce a very large amount of energy. Stars are big and contain a great deal of matter. So stars can give out energy for millions or billions of years before running out of nuclear fuel.

STUDYING THE STARS

An astronomer can learn about a star from studying the light it emits. To do this he uses instruments that spread the star's light out into a spectrum—a rainbow-like band of colors. The spectrum formed by the star's light has dark bands on it. The bands are produced by the chemical elements in the star. From these bands the astronomer can learn what elements are in the star, because he knows that each element always produces its own special bands on a spectrum. From a star's spectrum an astronomer may also learn the star's temperature.

Measuring Distance

If a star is less than 300 light-years away, astronomers can work out its distance from the earth. They observe the star from two positions that are a known—and very large—distance apart. For example, they may observe the star from opposite sides of the earth. Or they may make observations a half year apart, when the earth is at opposite sides of its path round the sun. In both cases the star appears to change its position. This apparent change in position is called *parallax*. By measuring a star's parallax, an astronomer can work out how far away the star is.

Astronomers often use Cepheid variables in working out the distance to groups of stars that are very far away. They have found that the time a Cepheid takes to grow dim and then bright again depends on the Cepheid's absolute magnitude. After observing a Cepheid, an astronomer can work out its absolute magnitude. By comparing its absolute and apparent magnitude, an astronomer can work out how far away it is. If the Cepheid is in a group of distant stars, then the astronomer also knows how far away that group of stars is.

Astronomers run into many problems when they observe stars. Some star motions, such as parallax, are not real motions. They are apparent motions, caused by the changing position of the earth in space. But stars also move. Sometimes it is hard to tell which motions are real and which are only apparent.

Despite such difficulties, astronomers have learned a great deal about stars. In recent years radio astronomy has opened up whole new areas. Using radio telescopes, astronomers can study the radio waves that the stars emit. Because of such new methods, man's knowledge about the universe and the behavior of the stars continues to grow.

Earth's Satellite—the Moon

The date: 20 July 1969. The place: the Sea of Tranquillity. The event: 'Here men from the planet earth first set foot upon the moon.' Man's first visit to a heavenly body other than his own planet was a great event. Logically, that visit was to the moon, earth's nearest neighbour in space.

The first men to walk on the moon used the lunar module (left) to ferry them from the command module. The earth shone out of a black sky in the background. Later, Buzz Aldrin stood on the Sea of Tranquillity (right).

The moon is the earth's only natural satellite. It travels round the earth at a speed of about 2,290 miles (3,664 kilometers) per hour. It orbits the earth once every 27 days or so.

The path it follows as it orbits the earth is not perfectly round. At times the moon comes close to the earth; at other times it is farther away. At its closest it is about 221,463 miles (354,336 kilometers) away, and is said to be at its *perigee*. At its farthest it is 252,710 miles (404,336 kilometers) away, and is said to be at its *apogee*.

HOW THE MOON CAME TO BE

How did the moon come into being? People have wondered about this for thousands of years.

Between mid-1969 and late 1972, six Apollo craft landed at various places on the moon. The Apollo astronauts conducted experiments and collected samples that have given us a much better knowledge of the moon. Scientists have now suggested new ideas about the way in which the moon and the earth might have begun and then evolved or changed with time.

Most scientists think that the moon, the earth and the other planets in the solar system originated at about the same time, 4,600,000,000 years ago. In fact, the Apollo 17 astronauts returned from the moon with rocks that were 4,600,000,000 years old. It is the oldest known rock other than meteorites (those solid lumps of matter from outer space that occasionally survive the friction of our atmosphere and lodge in the earth's crust).

The first stage in the development of the solar system may have been a vast cloud of gases and dust. As parts of the cloud cooled, they condensed into rock.

Some of the larger rocks, having more gravitational attraction, pulled other rocks towards them. In time, these ever-growing masses of rock collected to form the moon. The moon's growth was very violent. Huge and small rocks crashed onto the moon's surface. The energy of these crashes heated up the surface, melting the rocks. The moon's surface became a sea of glowing liquid rock (lava).

After many thousands of years fewer rocks fell on the moon, because there were fewer rocks left in space. The lava cooled slowly. Crystals of solid minerals formed in the cooling liquid. The crystals were not all alike. The lighter, or less dense ones, floated. In time they formed the moon's outer layer, or *crust*. The denser crystals sank, forming a lower layer of the moon, called the *mantle*.

After the crust cooled, some rocks continued to fall on the moon, blasting open huge craters in the solid crust and producing that familiar pitted appearance.

About 4,000,000,000 years ago, after the moon's outer crust was cool and solid, the mantle was heating up. This happened because the rocks in the deeper part of the moon contained radio-active elements such as uranium. A radio-active substance is unstable. The atoms of which it is composed break down at a constant rate. In one type of uranium, for example, the atoms break down to form atoms of another element, lead. Heat is produced during this process of radio-active decay.

The heat of radio-active decay built up within the moon until portions of the interior rocks melted to form lava. The heating up went on for millions of years. At last the lava worked its way up through the moon's crust. In some places the lava spilled across the surface, forming great plains. It also burst into the basins from below, in flow after flow of hot lava. These gigantic eruptions took place again and again, for a period of nearly 1,000,000,000 years. After they ended, about 3,000,000,000 years ago, the lava cooled. The rock that crystallized in the basins was mainly basalt. It was this dark, almost black rock, that led Galileo to call the basins 'maria', or 'seas', because it looked like water.

Except for the continuing impact of meteors, asteroids and comets, the moon has changed little since the last flows of basalt cooled. Great craters like Copernicus were formed during this 'quiet' time.

Most scientists now believe that the earth began and developed in the same general way and at the same time as the moon. But a great difference between the two bodies began to appear soon after the time of their formation. Millions of tons of nitrogen, carbon dioxide, water vapor and other gases formed a shell or blanket round the earth, held in place by the earth's gravity.

Over millions of years, as the earth's crust cooled, the water vapor condensed into drops of water and fell as rain. Torrents of water poured across the face of the earth. The rushing waters, violent winds and changes in the earth's crust itself, wore away the large craters and other evidence of the world's early history. It was the atmosphere and the oceans of water that made life on earth possible.

No atmosphere collected on the moon. Gases did not remain round it because its gravitational attraction was not strong enough to hold on to them. Without gases to provide an atmosphere or water, no great changes took place on the moon. The changes that have occurred in the last 3,000,000,000 years were caused mainly by asteroids, comets and meteors that crashed on the moon's surface. These objects dug out craters of all sizes.

For these billions of years the moon has looked much as we see it today. Its surface, cratered and mountainous, is like a partial portrait of our earth when it was young.

THE LUNAR WORLD

The diameter of the moon is 2,160 miles (3,456 kilometers), a quarter of that of the earth. The moon is quite a small satellite, as satellites go. But it is large compared with the size of the earth. Satellites are usually less than a quarter of the size of their parent planets (the planets they circle). For this reason, the earth and moon are often called a *double planetary system*; they are more like two planets circling each other than a large parent planet and a much smaller satellite.

The moon may appear to be perfectly round. But scientists have found that it has a slight bulge on the side that is turned towards the earth. They think that this is caused by the pull of the earth's gravity.

The Moving Moon

It takes the moon about 27 days to make a complete circle round the earth. As it travels in its orbit, it also spins round like a top. In the language of scientists, it rotates on its axis. One rotation takes 27 days, 7 hours and 43 minutes—about the same time that it takes for the moon to orbit the earth. As a result, the moon keeps the same side turned towards us all the time. And the moon moves in other ways, too. These movements, called *librations*, enable us to see a little more of the moon's surface.

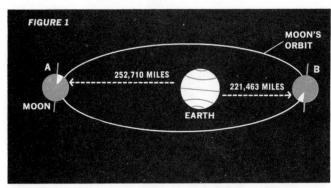

We can see a little more of the moon's surface (in white at A and B) because its axis is tilted.

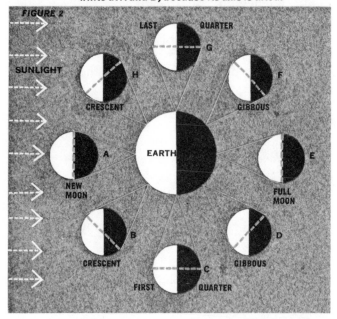

As the moon orbits the earth (above), its lighted side changes shape and size. The calendar (below) shows these changes, called phases, each month.

The moon is like a spinning top that leans over to one side slightly as it spins. Figure 1 will help you to understand this. The moon's axis, like the earth's, is tilted. When the moon is at (A) we can see an extra bit of the moon's surface, shown in white. When the moon is at (B) we can see another extra bit of surface.

Another kind of libration occurs because the moon's speed changes a little as it circles the earth. Although its orbiting speed changes, the speed at which it spins does not change. As a result, we can see a little more of the moon's surface.

Because of the librations, we can see about 59 per cent of the moon's surface at one time or another. But the other side of the moon was a complete mystery until 1959. Then an unmanned Russian space probe, Lunik III, circled the moon and sent back television pictures of the hidden side. Later, unmanned American and Russian moon probes and the Apollo astronauts were able to add greatly to this information.

New Moon, Full Moon

Unlike the sun and stars, the moon has no light of its own. Moonlight is really sunlight reflected from the moon's surface. The amount of sunlight that the moon reflects towards the earth varies. Sometimes we see a whole side of the moon lit up like a huge silver disc. At other times we see only a part of the lighted side. The shape that we see then is not a disc, but a crescent. These different shapes are called phases of the moon.

The phases occur because the moon orbits the earth, as Figure 2 shows. When the moon is at (A) the side facing us is in shadow. We cannot see the moon at all then. This phase is called *new moon*.

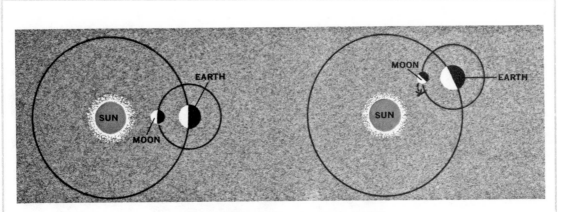

FROM NEW MOON TO NEW MOON

The moon takes a little over 27 days to make one trip round the earth. But the moon takes 29½ days to change from a new moon to the next new moon. There is a difference of more than 2 days between these two periods of time. You may think the times should be the same. But there is a reason for the difference.

The reason for the difference is that the earth moves round the sun while the moon moves round the earth. By the time the moon completes one orbit, the earth has moved farther in space. The moon has not quite reached its new-moon phase as yet. It must move a little farther round the earth before it is again between the earth and the sun. This extra distance accounts for the 2 extra days the moon takes to change from a new moon to the next new moon.

After 2 or 3 days the moon has moved on some distance. Now we can see just the thin edge of its lighted side. This is the *crescent moon* (B). The crescent waxes (grows) until, a week after new moon, we see half of the lighted side. This phase is known as the first quarter (C). It means that the moon has travelled through one-quarter of its orbit.

The moon moves on. We see a *gibbous moon* (D) when three-quarters of the side facing us is lit up and can be clearly seen. This is followed by the *full moon,* in which we can see the whole lighted disc.

After a day or two the full moon begins to wane (shrink). We see a gibbous phase (F), the last quarter (G) and then a crescent (H). Finally, we are back to new moon, a little more than 29½ days after the previous new moon.

How Eclipses Occur

While the moon circles the earth, the earth is continually travelling round the sun. As the earth and its moon travel together in their orbits round the sun, the moon sometimes passes directly between the sun and the earth. At other times, the earth comes between the sun and moon. This is the cause of eclipses.

When the moon passes between the sun and the earth, its shadow is thrown onto the earth. Over some areas of the earth, the sun is blotted out, and it seems like night. This type of eclipse is called a *solar eclipse,* or *eclipse of the sun,* because it is the sun that is hidden from view. During solar eclipses, the moon's shadow may measure from 60 miles (96 kilometers) to 160 miles (256 kilometers) across. It races over the earth at speeds of

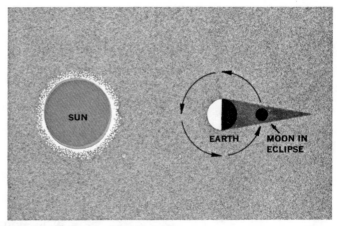

To produce the effect of a solar eclipse (left), let the shadow of a table tennis ball (moon) fall on a tennis ball (earth), partly eclipsing it. In a lunar eclipse (right) the moon darkens as it reaches the earth's shadow.

between 1,060 miles (1,696 kilometers) and 5,000 miles (8,000 kilometers) per hour.

When the earth passes directly between the sun and the moon, the moon is darkened by the earth's shadow for up to 3½ hours. The side that faces us, and which would normally reflect the sunlight back to earth, is completely hidden from sight. This is called a *lunar eclipse,* or *eclipse of the moon.*

The Moon's Gravity

If you have seen films of an astronaut on the moon, you may have been surprised by how easily he moved about. He carried on his back equipment that—on the earth—weighed 125 pounds (57 kilograms). Yet he could easily stride 6 feet (2 meters) or more. The secret lies in the difference between the gravity of the earth and that of the moon. The gravitational pull of the moon is only one-sixth that of the earth. A 175-pound (80-kilogram) astronaut and his 125-pound (57-kilogram) backpack weigh altogether only 50 pounds (23 kilograms) on the moon.

The moon's gravity—though it may seem weak—does have an effect on our earth. It causes the tides (the regular rising and falling of the world's oceans). Because of the movements of the sun and the moon, tides occur one hour later each day. The moon's gravity also creates tides in the atmosphere of earth—and even in the stuff of the earth itself.

STUDYING THE MOON

The study of the moon is not new. Greek astronomers accurately measured the size and distance of the moon more than 2,000 years ago. And the moon's movements have been studied for hundreds of years.

Galileo, the famous Italian astronomer, was the first man to turn his telescope on the moon. In 1609 he saw mountains and craters and dark, flat areas stretching over the moon's surface. He called the flat areas *maria* (singular, *mare*), the Latin word for 'seas'. We now know that these areas are not seas at all; they are as dry as the rest of the moon's surface.

Galileo drew the first rough map of the lunar surface. The first names given to the craters, mountains and 'seas' are still used today. There are craters called Copernicus, Plato and Julius Caesar. The 'seas' were given colorful names such as Oceanus Procellarum ('Ocean of Storms') and Mare Nubium ('Sea of Clouds'). Mare Tranquillitatis ('Sea of Tranquillity') was the landing place of Apollo 11—the first manned craft to land on the moon.

Mountains and Craters

With binoculars or a small telescope, you can see light and dark areas on the moon's surface. The highest mountains, rising to about 26,000 feet (8,000 meters) are clearly visible in the light areas. Some of them are in mountain chains, but most of them form the rims of craters.

Craters are flat, low-lying areas,

A magnified view of the moon's surface shows mountains, craters and rays.

roughly circular in shape. The largest of them are surrounded by high mountains. Smaller craters are ringed by hills, while the smallest are simply holes in the moon's surface.

Some of the larger craters are easy to see even without a telescope. One of the largest is Clavius, which is 145 miles (232 kilometers) across. The mountains that surround it are up to 17,000 feet (5,000 meters) high. Hundreds of other giant craters are known.

Photographs taken through powerful telescopes have shown many thousands of small craters—some only a few hundred feet wide. The close-up pictures taken by moon probes have revealed millions of these tiny craters. Neil Armstrong and Edwin Aldrin, the first men on the moon, saw thousands of craters measuring between 3 feet and 50 feet (1 meter to 15 meters) in width.

Mountains often form a circular wall round the longer craters. Outside the crater they slope down gently to the surrounding surface. But inside, they slope steeply to the flat central plain. In most craters the central plain is lower than the surface outside the crater, sometimes by as much as 10,000 feet (3,000 meters).

In some craters the central plain is smooth. Other craters have one or more mountains rising from inside them. These mountains are usually near the center of the crater. For example, the crater Copernicus has seven mountain peaks near its center. A crater's central moun-

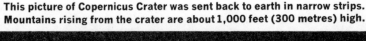

This picture of Copernicus Crater was sent back to earth in narrow strips. Mountains rising from the crater are about 1,000 feet (300 metres) high.

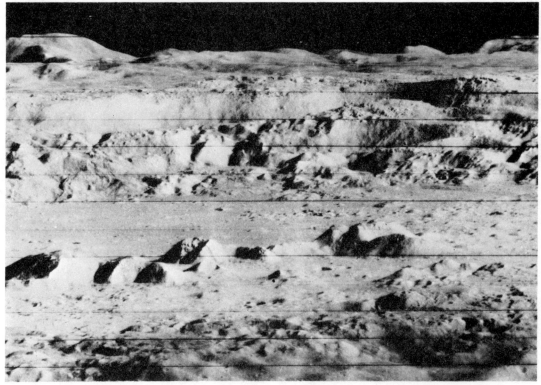

tains are not as high as the surrounding mountain wall. The central peak in the crater Theophilus, for example, is 7,000 feet (2,000 meters) high, but the mountainous rim of the crater is 18,000 feet (5,400 meters) high.

How Were the Craters Formed?

Craters are formed on earth in one of two ways. They may be the result of volcanic action, when molten rock from inside the earth forced its way to the surface and left a crater at each point of exit. Or they may be scars of collisions between the earth and meteors—lumps of rock that occasionally fall from space. There are similar theories about the craters on the moon. Some scientists believe that most of the craters were formed by volcanic activity (the 'hot moon' theory). Others think that meteoric collisions caused them (the 'cold moon' theory).

According to the 'hot moon' theory, the craters were formed when the moon was young. Hot molten rock under pressure lay beneath the thin layer of rock that formed the moon's crust. The molten rock burst through the crust again and again, building up areas of high land. After a time, the centres of the volcanoes collapsed, leaving only low-lying craters ringed by the mountains that once formed the rim of the volcanoes. Later still, new outbreaks formed the central peaks seen in some craters. The volcanic action finally came to an end, leaving the moon cold and dead—or so it seems.

Some astronomers have reported seeing bright flashes of color on the moon. Others report what looks like masses of cloud in the crater Alphonsus. Pictures taken through telescopes and by the Ranger IX moon probe show curious

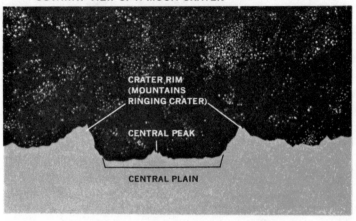

CUTAWAY VIEW OF A MOON CRATER

CRATER RIM (MOUNTAINS RINGING CRATER)

CENTRAL PEAK

CENTRAL PLAIN

smaller craters within Alphonsus. These are surrounded by dark areas, which may be made up of volcanic material from recent eruptions. Perhaps the moon is not dead after all.

According to the meteoric theory the moon was bombarded by enormous meteors about 3,000,000,000 years ago. Each meteor smashed out a huge crater on the lunar surface. Rocks thrown up by these collisions fell back, forming smaller craters. Some meteors fell close together, so that overlapping craters were formed. Small meteors still fall on the moon forming new craters. Even the scientists who support the volcanic theory agree that the smaller craters are made by meteors.

The Apollo astronauts may help to clear up the mystery of the lunar craters. The visitors from the earth left seismometers on the surface of the moon. These instruments can pick up moonquakes and other disturbances in the ground and report them by radio to scientists on earth. The astronauts also brought back to earth collections of lunar rocks. These rocks and the seismometer records may help scientists to decide whether the moon is a 'hot moon,

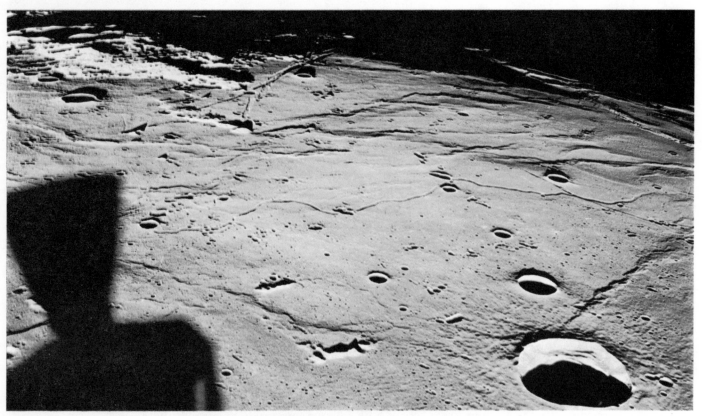

This picture of the moon's surface, was taken by Apollo 11 astronauts
Armstrong and Aldrin from a height of 63 miles (101 kilometers).
It clearly shows several craters and the shadow of the lunar module.

a 'cold moon' or both. The study may provide new information about the age and history of the whole solar system.

Cracks and Wrinkles

One feature of the moon's surface that has puzzled scientists are the pale streaks, called *rays*. They look like the spokes of a wheel stretching away for hundreds of miles from certain craters. The most noticeable rays stretch from the crater Tycho. Some of them are 1,500 miles (2,400 kilometers) long.

One theory is that the rays are cracks formed by the shrinking of the moon's surface. But cracks would be in shadow, and, therefore, darker in color than the surrounding land. According to another theory, the rays were formed from dust thrown up by meteors as they fell on the moon.

Powerful telescopes on earth, lunar probes, and the Apollo astronauts have photographed another strange feature of the moon's surface. This is made up of what looks like long narrow valleys called *rilles*. Some rilles are straight; others twist and turn their way over the moon's surface. Scientists think that the straight rilles may be breaks, or faults, in the moon's crust. There are many faults on the earth's surface—the result of great pressure building up beneath the earth's crust. Such faults cause most of the quakes and tremors we experience on earth.

The origin of the twisty rilles is a mystery. Some scientists believe they were formed when the moon had water and an atmosphere. Flowing water cut the rilles, as it cuts river valleys on the earth. Then the water evaporated, leaving the dry rilles. Other scientists suggest that flows of lava formed the rilles.

The Moon's 'Seas'

Galileo thought that the flat, dark areas on the moon were seas because they looked quite smooth. Today we know that the seas are dry. And they are certainly not smooth. Large craters are found there along with millions of small ones. When the Apollo 11 astronauts landed on the Sea of Tranquillity, they had to change course at the last moment to avoid one of the craters that scar its surface.

Craters on the lunar seas are a problem for astronauts, and so are the seas themselves. Space scientists have noted a strange feature of some of the moon's round seas. They have a stronger gravitational pull on satellites and spaceships than other parts of the moon.

The gravitational pull of an object depends on the amount of matter, or mass, in the object. Scientists reason that the stronger pull of the circular seas is explained by a greater collection or concentration, of mass in them. The words 'mass' and 'concentration' have been shortened to *mascons,* meaning concentrations of mass. The mascons are a great problem for astronauts preparing to land on the moon. They can pull a spacecraft off course. These changes in course must be worked out in advance and allowed for if the craft is to land at the chosen place on the moon.

How were the lunar seas formed? One theory explains them as flows of lava that have cooled and hardened. Imagine a giant meteor falling onto the moon. It gouges out an enormous, roughly circular crater. The force of the collision cracks the moon's crust and lava from below flows up to fill the newly-formed crater. The lava spreads out—completely covering the meteor—and cools. It hardens to a flat surface. The heavy meteorite, buried under the lighter lava, might then act as a mascon.

There is another theory about the lunar seas. According to this, the moon once had water and an atmosphere, as the earth does today. Great craters dug by meteors formed the basins into which the rivers flowed, as rivers on the earth flow into ocean basins. Like earthly rivers, the lunar rivers carried grains of rock, or sediment. The sediment settled in the seas over a period of many millions of years, forming thick layers of rock. As this process continued, the water of the moon turned into gas or vapor, uncovering the heavy rocks. These rocks are the mascons. The rivers that emptied into the lunar seas no longer flow. But the river beds can still be seen in the form of twisting rilles.

A WORLD WITHOUT AIR

When scientists were planning to land men on the moon they had to provide a way for them to breathe because there is no atmosphere on the moon. Astronomers knew this from the many observations that they had made.

Scientists had noticed that there was no twilight on the moon. On earth, day changes slowly to night because the atmosphere of the earth reflects the sun's light, even after the sun has sunk below the horizon. On the moon there is light one moment, and the next moment it is night. Astronomers never see any mists or clouds on the moon. They would expect to see both if the moon had an atmosphere.

There is another way of showing that the moon is airless. Astronomers observe a star as the moon passes in front of it. The star remains clearly visible until the moment it disappears behind the moon. If air surrounded the moon, the star's light would gradually grow dimmer as it passed through an ever-thickening layer of air.

Many kinds of rays are constantly travelling through space. They make up what is known as radiation. The heat and light of the sun are two forms of radiation. Life on the earth depends on them. But there are other kinds of radiation that are a danger to life. Some of them come from the sun; others come from far out in space.

Our earth's atmosphere filters out most of the dangerous radiation before it reaches us. But the moon, without a protective blanket of air, receives radiation of all kinds—radiation that would destroy life. Spacecraft and space suits must, therefore, be designed to shield astronauts from radiation.

Moon explorers may also have trouble with rocks falling from outer space. Have you ever seen a bright trail left by a meteor in the night sky? The trail shows the path of a piece of rock falling to earth from outer space. These pieces, most of which are very small, approach the earth at speeds of up to 30 miles (48 kilometers) a second. When they enter the earth's atmosphere, the resistance of the air through which they pass causes them to become hot. They get so hot that they burn up before they hit the earth. All that remains, in most cases, is

a fine powder that floats gently to earth. But sometimes the meteors are so large that comparatively small pieces of solid rock survive their passage through the atmosphere to hit the earth. These pieces are called meteorites.

On the moon, there is no atmosphere to destroy the meteors that rain in from space. Meteors, large and small, are constantly bombarding the moon's surface. Indeed, this may be the cause of the craters that we can see on the moon.

The earth's atmosphere performs another life-giving function on earth. It spreads the sun's heat over the whole surface of the globe. Hot areas near the equator are cooled by cold air that flows from the north and south poles. And the poles, in turn, are heated by warm air travelling from the equator. On the moon there are no winds to spread the intense heat of the sun over the surface.

As a result, the moon's sunny side is heated to more than 120° C (250° F)—hotter than boiling water. The lunar day lasts for two of our weeks. It is followed by two weeks of night when the temperature falls to −161° C (−260° F). There is no form of life as we know it that could survive these enormous temperature changes. Spacecraft and space suits must have special air-conditioning machinery built into them to protect the wearer from both heat and cold.

The atmosphere even affects the color of the sky. An astronaut on the moon sees a very different sky from the one you see. To him it looks black, even in daytime. On the earth the sun's light is scattered and reflected by the air. This makes the sky look blue. On the moon and in outer space there is no air to scatter the light. In the black skies over the moon and in outer space, sun and stars can be seen shining at the same time.

Rockets—Space-Age Engines

Rockets date back to 13th-century China. The Chinese made them out of tubes of bamboo or heavy paper. These tubes were closed at one end and filled with gunpowder (which the Chinese also invented). They then lashed the tubes to arrows, and when the gunpowder was set alight, it would speed the arrows toward the enemy. These were the first rocket missiles.

Strickly speaking, rockets and missiles are not the same thing. The word rocket really refers to a special kind of engine. A missile, on the other hand, is any object that is forcefully sent towards a target. When people talk about missiles, they usually mean rockets that carry explosives or 'warheads'.

HOW DO ROCKETS WORK?

You can see for yourself how rockets work. Put a garden hose on a fairly smooth surface, and turn the water on full force. Adjust the nozzle until you get the most powerful jet. See how the hose twists and turns as the water rushing out forces the nozzle backwards. Rockets work on the same principle. The action of the rushing gas coming out of the open end of a rocket causes the container to move in the opposite direction.

Rockets Need Special Fuel

The amount of fuel that a rocket burns each second gives a rocket its power. The kind of fuel burned also affects power.

Some fuels produce more thrust than others. The most energetic rocket fuel known is hydrogen. Hydrogen is the lightest of all gases. A gas is not suitable as a rocket fuel, however, because it takes up too much space. For use as a rocket fuel, hydrogen is compressed until it becomes a liquid. Because it is so cold in liquid form, hydrogen is very difficult to handle, even with the greatest care. It is also very expensive. Therefore, it is used in rockets only when its high energy is absolutely necessary.

There are several hydrogen-rich fuels that are liquid at ordinary temperatures. Two important ones are kerosene and hydrazine. Certain hydrogen-rich solids are also used as fuels. Some types of rubber and plastics are such solids.

'Lox' and 'Flox'

Rockets are the only engines that can operate in outer space. In order to burn, fuels must combine with a type of chemical called an *oxidizer*. Oxygen is the most common oxidizer. Large quantities of oxygen are present in the air. Airplanes take in air and use its oxygen to burn their fuel. But rockets carry their own oxidizer, in liquid or solid form, inside their cases. They do not need oxygen from the air.

Pure oxygen is one of the best oxidizers to use because it is so energetic and it readily combines with fuels. In liquid form, pure oxygen is called *lox*, from

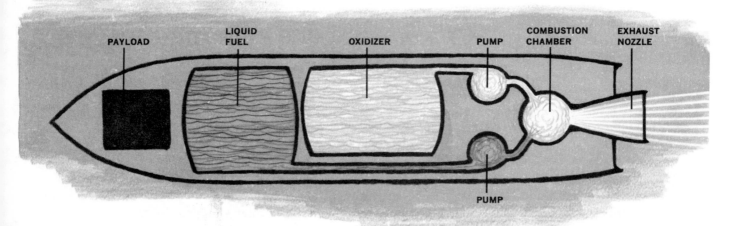

PAYLOAD   LIQUID FUEL   OXIDIZER   PUMP   COMBUSTION CHAMBER   EXHAUST NOZZLE

PUMP

In a liquid-fuel rocket, pumps drive the fuel and oxidizer into the combustion chamber.

the first letters of 'liquid' and 'oxygen'. Lox is frequently used as the oxidizer in liquid-fuel rockets.

Fluorine is a better oxidizer than pure oxygen. But fluorine is dangerous and very hard to work with. At present, scientists are able to use only a little liquid fluorine, which they add to lox to make an 'oxidizer-fluoridizer' called *flox* (fluorine-lox).

Lox and flox cannot be stored very long in a rocket. One reason for this is that they boil constantly, turning back into a gas. Rockets that use them must be 'loxed' or 'floxed' at the last moment before launching.

Other oxidizers, in both solid and liquid form, are also used. The combination of a fuel and an oxidizer is called a *bi-propellant*, or simply *propellant*. In general, liquid propellants produce a greater thrust than solid propellants.

Solid and Liquid Propellants

The rocket engineer chooses propellants according to the job the rocket is to do. He usually chooses a solid propellant for small military rockets. Rockets that use solid propellants can be fuelled, then stored for long periods of time.

In fuelling a solid-propellant rocket, the fuel and oxidizer are first mixed together outside the rocket. While still soft, the mixture is poured into the rocket case round a form set into the case. The fuel hardens inside the case. The form is then pulled out, leaving a hole in the solid fuel. The size and shape of the hole left in the mixture determines how fast the fuel will burn.

Most solid fuels are not as energetic as liquid fuels. But solid-fuel rockets can be ready for action at all times. Most military rockets use solid fuels. But some use a special type of liquid propellant that can be stored in the rocket. The rocket can then be fuelled and kept ready for action.

Different liquid propellants are used if the rocket does not need to be ready at all times and if it needs exceptionally great power. Such rockets, for example, are used to put a spacecraft into orbit. These are fuelled just before launching.

Liquid-propellant rockets are more difficult to design and operate than solid-propellant rockets. One reason for this is that liquid-propellant rockets have a complicated system of tanks, pumps, valves and pipes. The liquid fuel and the oxidizer must be carried in separate tanks. Hoses and pumps are needed to feed the liquids to the rocket engines.

ROCKET STAGES

A single enormous rocket could be built to carry a heavy payload (whatever a rocket carries is called its 'payload'). But it would not be economical or efficient, because the weight of the fuel and the fuel tanks would be very great. Tremendous thrust would be needed to lift such a rocket and accelerate it to the proper speed.

A rocket needs the most thrust at launching. Once started, the rocket becomes lighter as its propellants are burned. This means that there is a constant decrease in the amount of weight the thrust must accelerate, so the rocket gains speed very quickly.

After a few seconds of flight a rocket's fuel tanks are no longer full. But the tanks themselves are very heavy. The empty parts of the tanks are unnecessary weight in a rocket.

Rocket engineers have solved the problem of useless rocket weight after take-off. They mount the rockets on top of each other. The smallest rocket is on top, and the largest rocket is at the bottom. The bottom rocket is the main launching rocket. This method of mounting rockets is called *staging*, and each rocket is called a *stage*. Each stage is complete with its own engine and propellants. The combination of stages is called a *multi-stage rocket*. The main launching rocket is called the first stage or *booster*. The next stage is called the second stage, and so on to the topmost rocket, which is called the final, or upper stage.

The booster is cut loose when it has used up all its fuel, usually within 2 minutes. The engines of the second

rocket stage then begin to fire. When its fuel is used up, it, too, is cut loose and the engines of the third stage start firing.

Each stage is lighter in weight than the one before it. It carries less fuel because it needs less thrust to accelerate it. And each stage goes faster than the one before it because of constant acceleration. The last stage goes the fastest and the farthest.

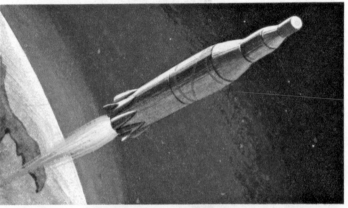

Above: When a multi-stage rocket is launched, the largest engine (the first stage) provides the power.

Above: The first stage is cast off when emptied of fuel. Below: The second stage is cast off. The final stage sends the rocket to its destination.

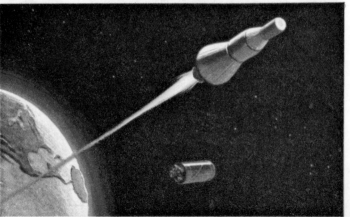

Steering a Rocket

Steering devices in most modern rockets are operated by 'command'. This means that they may be started and stopped by radio or radar signals beamed to the rocket from the ground. 'Command' may also mean that the steering devices are set before the rocket is launched.

The commands may be pre-programmed—that is, they may be put on special magnetic tape. As the tape unwinds, it sends signals to the steering controls. The tape may be connected to a clock that gives the signals at the proper time.

One type of command is called *inertial command* or *inertial guidance*. In this type, gyroscopes (wheels that turn freely in all directions) are placed in the rocket when it is built. These gyroscopes are able to sense any change in the rocket's direction. Each change is changed into an electric signal. The signal sends corrections to the steering mechanism.

In some command systems, information from gyroscopes and other devices in the rocket is sent to a computer at the ground station. The computer works out what steering corrections should be made. It then sends the corrections to the steering apparatus by radio or radar beam.

NEW FORMS OF PROPULSION

Scientists are developing rockets that will use electrical or nuclear energy. These rockets will no doubt be much more efficient than those using chemical propellants.

One form of electric propulsion is the ion engine. The fuel used is mercury or caesium. The atoms of the fuels are changed into charged particles called ions. Electromagnets accelerate the ions to tremendous speeds. The ions rush out through the exhaust nozzles of the rocket, giving the rocket its power.

The big advantage of this kind of rocket is that it needs very little fuel to operate.

There is a disadvantage, however. It does not have enough thrust to lift it off a launching pad. This means that it must be launched by a powerful booster rocket, or that it must start its journey from an artificial satellite already in orbit. Once it is moving, it gains speed gradually. It may take a few months of travel to reach its greatest speed. But it can continue at that speed for years.

It is also possible to obtain rocket power from a small nuclear reactor. One type of nuclear rocket of the future will use liquid hydrogen as a fuel. A nuclear reactor produces great amounts of heat. The heat of the rocket's reactor is used to turn the hydrogen into a very hot, energetic gas. The hot hydrogen gas rushes out through the exhaust nozzles and gives the rocket its power.

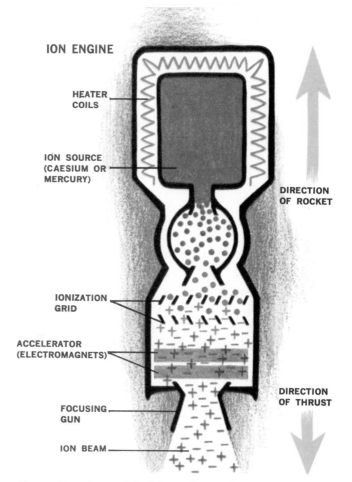

ION ENGINE

HEATER COILS

ION SOURCE (CAESIUM OR MERCURY)

IONIZATION GRID

ACCELERATOR (ELECTROMAGNETS)

FOCUSING GUN

ION BEAM

DIRECTION OF ROCKET

DIRECTION OF THRUST

Above: The atoms of fuel in an ion engine are changed to ions at the grid. The ions are first accelerated, then focused so that they shoot out of the exhaust. Below: Powerful rockets were needed to ensure the success of the Apollo moon landings.

A Workshop in the Sky

In recent years the people of the world have watched men land and walk on the moon. There will not be another manned flight to the moon for a long while. But in 1973 a new phase of space exploration began. On 14 May of that year, the United States launched Skylab, an earth-orbiting space station as big as a 10-storey building. During 1973 and early 1974, three teams of American astronauts lived and worked in Skylab as it circled 270 miles (435 kilometers) above the surface of the earth.

Can men remain in space for long periods and perform useful work while they are there? It was basically to answer this question that the Skylab missions were undertaken. During space flights men do not experience the force of gravity as they do on earth: their bodies are weightless. What would be the effects of such weightlessness during a long space flight—a trip to Mars, for example? Such a trip there and back would take almost a year. Much needs to be learned about the medical effects of

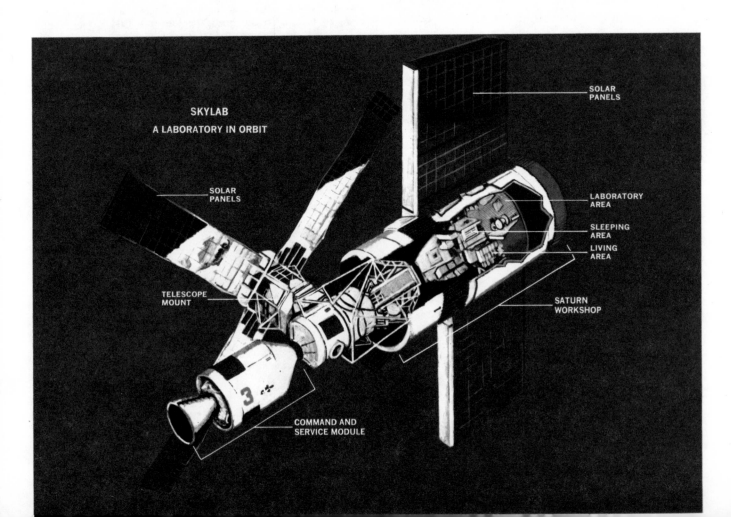

SKYLAB
A LABORATORY IN ORBIT

SOLAR PANELS

SOLAR PANELS

LABORATORY AREA

SLEEPING AREA

LIVING AREA

TELESCOPE MOUNT

SATURN WORKSHOP

COMMAND AND SERVICE MODULE

Skylab I orbits the earth. As you can see by comparing this photograph with the illustration on the opposite page, one solar wing, or panel, is missing.

prolonged weightlessness if men are ever to travel to Mars or to other planets.

Another aim of Skylab was to explore the practical and scientific value of having men orbit the earth. The Skylab astronauts performed many experiments and studies as they orbited high above the earth. They collected information about the earth's resources, ecology (the relationship of living things to their surroundings and to each other) and weather. They made studies of the sun and the stars. These studies could not have been made from the earth because of the interference of the earth's atmosphere.

THE FIRST MEN IN SKYLAB

Skylab, the space station itself, was launched on 14 May 1973. The Skylab II astronauts were supposed to be sent up the next day, but trouble forced a change of plan.

Just after Skylab's launch, as the space station raced through the earth's upper atmosphere, an aluminium shield tore off. This accident caused major problems. First, the orbiting spacecraft overheated. The aluminium shield was designed to reflect the sun's rays. Without its protection, the space station became very hot. If scientists could not find a way to cool off Skylab, the mission would have to be abandoned.

The second problem was that the accident disabled two great solar wings. These wings were to open after Skylab went into orbit. They were to convert sunlight into electricity, and without them Skylab would be cut off from its major source of electrical power.

Because of this accident, the launching of the first crew was postponed several times. Meanwhile, scientists worked on a number of possible procedures for the astronauts to try when they reached Skylab. Finally, on 25 May, the Skylab

II astronauts were launched. They were Captain Charles Conrad, Jr., Commander Joseph P. Kerwin and Commander Paul J. Weitz.

The astronauts blasted off in a spacecraft similar to the one used in the Apollo moon program. Their aim was to dock with the orbiting space station. When the astronauts neared Skylab, they saw that one solar wing had been ripped away. The second wing, however, was only jammed so that it could not open. As he stood in the hatch of the Apollo craft, Weitz used a long shepherd's crook to try to free the jammed wing. But he could not do it. Then came another problem: the astronauts found it difficult to dock Skylab II with Skylab I. They needed ten tries before they made a firm docking.

The astronauts slept that first night in the Apollo capsule. The next day they entered Skylab. They found it as hot as expected and quickly set about to solve the problem. The solution was a space 'parasol'. Scientists on earth had built a great parasol-like device of metal and fiber. The closed parasol was pushed out through a hatchway. It was then opened, in much the same way as you would open an umbrella. The device worked. It shielded Skylab from the sun's rays, and the temperature inside the space station began to fall. Within a few days, the astronauts were able to move into Skylab.

The astronauts were also able to free Skylab's jammed solar wing. In a daring space walk, Conrad and Kerwin used shears to cut a metal strip that was preventing the solar wing from opening. Now there would be enough electrical power to complete their scheduled 28 days in space.

During the Skylab III mission, Arabella spins a web and Alan Bean weighs himself.

On 22 June the astronauts returned to earth. How would they react to earth's gravity after 28 days in space? After shorter flights some American astronauts and Soviet cosmonauts had experienced great weakness and fatigue. The fact that the Skylab astronauts were able to walk unaided out of their capsule was an encouraging sign. But the three men did suffer from some dizziness, nausea, fatigue and low blood pressure after landing. Because of this, doctors recommended more exercise for the astronauts of the Skylab III and IV missions.

SKYLAB III AND SKYLAB IV

Captain Alan L. Bean, Major Jack R. Lousma and Dr. Owen K. Garriott, a civilian scientist, formed the second team of astronauts to live and work in Skylab. They were launched on 28 July. Their mission was very successful, and the Skylab III crew spent a record 59 days in space.

The Skylab III astronauts circled the earth 859 times during their two months in orbit. They returned to earth with about 77,000 photographs of the sun. These were taken through an array of telescopes mounted outside Skylab. They also brought back a great deal of information about the earth and its environment, including some 17,000 photographs.

Some of the Skylab III experiments were suggested by students. One interesting experiment tested whether spiders could weave webs in the weightlessness of outer space. Two spiders, Anita and Arabella, were carried into space with the astronauts. For two days the spiders seemed confused by the absence of gravity. But then they adapted to their new surroundings and began to weave webs. The experiment seemed to indicate that animals have a basic ability to adapt to

Skylab III astronaut Jack Lousma walks in space.

weightlessness. This finding seems to promise well for man's future in space.

The Skylab III astronauts did more exercise during their mission than the Skylab II astronauts had done. It seems that the increase in exercise worked. When the crew returned to earth, on 25 September, they were in better shape than the Skylab II crew had been.

Skylab IV, the third mission to Skylab, was the longest of all—84 days. Lieutenant-Colonels Gerald P. Carr and William R. Pogue and Dr. Edward G. Gibson blasted off on 16 November 1973. They returned to earth on 8 February 1974.

The Skylab IV astronauts orbited the earth 1,213 times. They took more than 20,000 photographs of the earth, the sun and solar phenomena. They also collected a great deal of information on the earth's natural resources, as well as on weather and crops. During December and January, the astronauts also studied the comet Kohoutek.

The astronauts, who had made four space walks during their mission, were in excellent physical condition when they returned to earth.

Skylab ended its six-year orbit on July 11, 1979. As the space station re-entered the earth's atmosphere it broke up into millions of fragments. Pieces of Skylab were scattered over a 4,000-mile (6,700-kilometer) trail across the Indian Ocean and the scrublands of central Australia.

The Russians have also placed space stations in orbit, and in mid-1975 there was an orbital link-up of an American Apollo spacecraft and a Russian Soyuz space-craft.

Some scientists are suggesting that in the next century there will be space communities—people living in space (between the moon and the earth) in giant cylinders 16 miles (26 kilometers) long.

Does this sound like science fiction? Perhaps. But not too many years ago Skylab—the workshop in the sky—would have been considered science fiction.

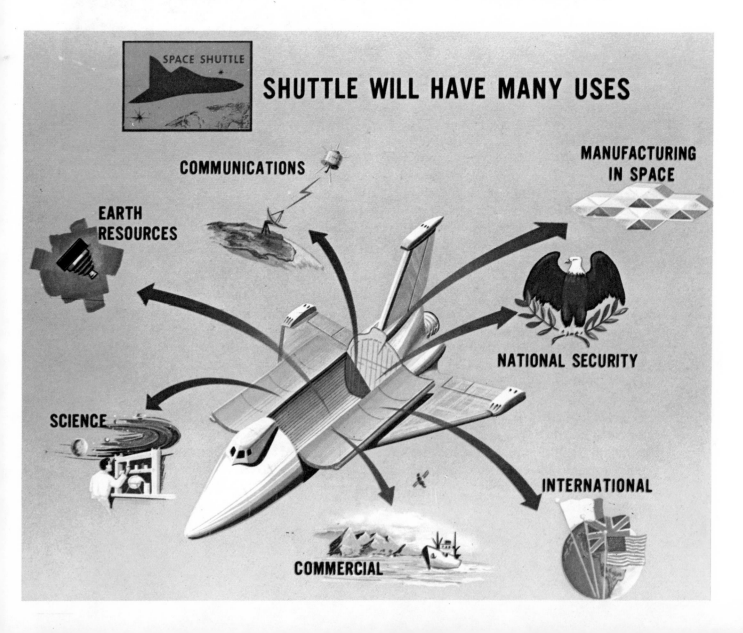

SPACE SHUTTLE

SHUTTLE WILL HAVE MANY USES

COMMUNICATIONS

MANUFACTURING IN SPACE

EARTH RESOURCES

NATIONAL SECURITY

SCIENCE

INTERNATIONAL

COMMERCIAL

To the Moon and Beyond

For centuries man has dreamed of leaving the planet Earth to explore the unknown mysteries of space. Journeys to the moon and beyond have long been the subject of science fiction. In 1969, with man setting foot on the moon, fiction became reality.

The dawn of the Space Age, however, came 12 years before the moon landing—on 4 October 1957. On that day the Soviet Union launched Sputnik 1, the world's first artificial earth-orbiting satellite. The United States launched its first artificial satellite, Explorer 1, on 31 January 1958. With these two launch-ings, it was clear that the Soviet Union and the United States both planned to place a man in orbit round the earth.

The American effort to place a man in orbit was called Project Mercury. The first production Mercury space capsule was flown unmanned in December 1960. A chimpanzee named Ham was flown in a Mercury capsule in January 1961. Then, in May 1961, Alan Shepard made a sub-orbital flight to become the United States' first man in space. A sub-orbital flight is one that goes into space and returns to earth, but does not go into orbit.

Space pioneers: Ham, the astrochimp (below), made a sub-orbital flight in 1961. Russian cosmonaut Yuri Gagarin (right) was the first man to orbit the earth; he was lifted aloft by a Vostok rocket (far right). Alan Shepard (below, center) was the first American in space.

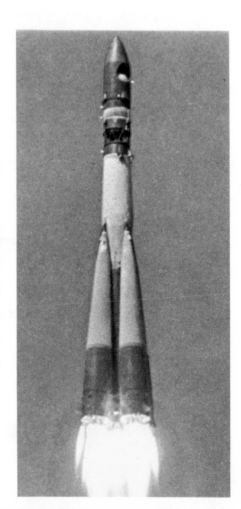

In December 1965 Gemini 6 and Gemini 7 made space history by rendezvousing in space. At one point the two spacecraft were only 6 feet apart.

service modules and the lunar module, or lunar lander. It was planned that three astronauts would make the trip from earth orbit to moon orbit. Once in moon orbit, two of the astronauts would enter the lunar lander and pilot it to the surface of the moon. The third astronaut would stay in the command module. After a period of time on the moon, the two astronauts would pilot the lunar lander from the moon back to the command module. They would then make the long trip back to earth.

Plans for the moon landing were well advanced by 1965. An important part of these plans was Project Gemini. The purpose of this project was to gain the flight experience and the advanced technology needed for the mission to the moon.

In December 1965 two astronauts aboard the spacecraft Gemini 7 orbited

Shepard's flight, for example, reached an altitude of 116.5 miles (187.5 kilometers), and only 15 minutes elapsed between blast-off and splash-down.

One month before Shepard's flight, Soviet Cosmonaut Yuri Gagarin orbited the earth aboard the spacecraft Vostok I. He was the world's first space traveller.

PREPARING FOR
THE MOON SHOT

On 25 May 1961, United States President John F. Kennedy announced that the Americans would try to land a man on the moon before 1970. Within one year of this decision, the master plan for the lunar landing—called the Apollo Program—was worked out. The first part of the plan called for a giant, 3-stage Saturn rocket to boost an Apollo spacecraft into earth orbit. The Apollo spacecraft would consist of command and

Gemini 4 astronaut Edward White was the first American to walk in space. The first man to walk in space was Aleksei Leonov, a Russian cosmonaut.

40

While the Americans were preparing to land a man on the moon, the Russians were preparing to land the Lunokhod, an unmanned lunar vehicle.

the earth for 14 days. This flight showed that man could fly in space in a weightless condition for more than ten days—the time required to fly to the moon and back. At the same time, two astronauts aboard Gemini 6 manœuvred their spacecraft to within 1 foot of Gemini 7. Docking of two spacecraft was first done by the astronauts in Gemini 8. On 16 March 1966 they docked their spacecraft to an unmanned target vehicle.

Another goal of the Gemini Project was to give the astronauts experience outside the spacecraft. The first American astronaut to do this was Colonel Edward White. On 3 June 1965 White ventured out of the Gemini 4 capsule for a 20-minute walk in space. Three months earlier, a Russian cosmonaut had become the first man to walk in space.

Mapping the Moon

The plan to land men on the moon was progressing quite well. But before men could actually land there, certain questions had to be answered. Was the moon's surface safe for landings? Was it solid enough to support the weight of a spacecraft? Or was it covered with thick layers of dust that would swallow up men and machines?

To learn more about the moon with no risk to human life, Russian and American scientists launched several kinds of unmanned moon probes. In 1959 a Russian craft took close-up pictures of the moon—some of them of the moon's hidden side. The American Ranger probes were designed to photograph the moon as they fell towards it. They continued to send pictures back to earth until they crashed

The lunar module was designed to carry two astronauts from the command module to the moon and back. It is shown here being tested in earth orbit.

on to the moon's surface. In 1964 and 1965 the last three Rangers sent back more than 17,000 pictures.

After the Rangers, other types of craft were sent to investigate the moon. Lunar Orbiter probes swooped down to within 25 miles (40 kilometers of the moon's surface. The pictures they sent back to earth were used to choose landing sites for the later manned Apollo spacecraft. The Lunar Orbiters also taught us about the moon's size, shape and gravitational pull.

In 1966 the Surveyor probes actually began to land on the moon. The most successful of these landed on the moon's surface near the crater Tycho. It was fitted with a television camera and a mechanical scoop—both following commands radioed from earth. The pictures of the little ditches it dug told scientists what the moon's surface in that area was like. It was like damp soil—strong enough to support the Apollo astronauts and their lunar lander.

THE APOLLO PROGRAM

The Apollo spacecraft, which carried American astronauts to the moon and back, are made up of three sections, or modules. These are the command module (CM), the service module (SM) and the lunar module (LM).

The command module houses the astronauts. It also contains the instruments and controls for operating the spacecraft and communicating with earth. It is the only part of the spacecraft that returns to earth. The command module is sometimes called the 'capsule'.

The service module is below the command module. Its rocket engine can be started and stopped as needed. Its push, or thrust, slows the craft as it approaches the moon and starts the Apollo capsule

This photograph of the far side of the moon was taken by the Apollo 10 astronauts.

back towards the earth on the return trip. The service module holds the electrical power system for the craft and the fuel for the rocket engine.

The third part of the Apollo spacecraft is the strange-looking lunar module. It is sometimes called the 'bug' because it has four spidery legs. The legs are folded during the flight, and are extended before the moon landing. The lunar module is really two spacecraft. The lower part, which has the legs, is the descent stage. Its rocket engine's thrust is downward. This thrust enables the lunar module to settle gently on to the moon's surface. The upper part of the lunar module is the ascent stage. The astronauts stand in this part. It has its own rocket engine. When the astronauts are ready to leave the moon, this engine fires. Its thrust pushes the ascent stage upward, leaving the descent stage behind. The ascent stage rises straight up for a few seconds, then tilts to follow a course that will carry it to meet the orbiting command and service modules.

Round the Moon

In December 1968, the Americans were ready for the first manned flight to the moon. But this flight was not designed to land on the moon. Rather, it was designed to fly to the moon, go into lunar orbit, take pictures of the lunar landing sites and then return to earth. This flight was Apollo 8. Aboard it, three astronauts made man's first trip to the moon. The craft circled the moon ten times at an altitude of 70 miles (112 kilometers). It then returned to earth.

The way for this historic flight had been paved by the Apollo 7 flight, which took place two months earlier. Aboard Apollo 7, three astronauts orbited the earth in the Apollo command and service modules for 11 days. This was the first manned flight in the Apollo Program.

Apollo 8 was followed in March 1969

Apollo 11 astronaut Edwin Aldrin, Jr, climbs onto the surface of the moon. The photograph was taken by astronaut Neil Armstrong, first man to walk on the moon.

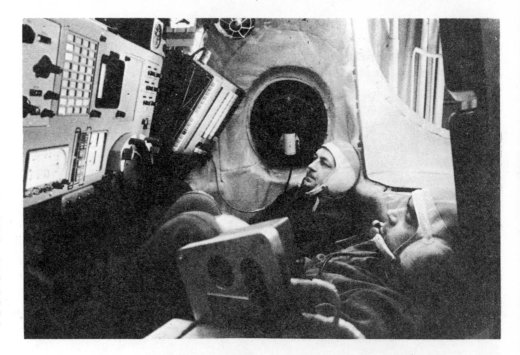

During 1970, the Apollo Program suffered a setback when the Apollo 13 command module was damaged by an explosion. The astronauts were forced to abandon plans to land on the moon. The Russians however, made great strides in 1970. In Soyuz 9, two cosmonauts (right) set a manned space-flight record of nearly 18 days. Luna 16 (below) travelled to the moon, retrieved soil from the lunar surface and returned to earth.

by Apollo 9. This flight tested, in earth orbit, the lunar module and the command and service modules. This was the first manned flight of the lunar module. Rendezvous and docking between the command and service modules and the lunar module were also tested.

The Americans were now ready for the final dress rehearsal for the lunar-landing mission. Apollo 10 was launched in May 1969. It went through all the phases of the lunar-landing mission except the actual landing. Two astronauts piloted their lunar module to 9·26 miles (14·9 kilometers) above the lunar surface. They then rendezvoused with the command module and returned to earth. By July 1969 all the preparations had been made for the landing on the moon.

Man On the Moon

Apollo 11 was launched on the morning of 16 July 1969. The landing on the moon was made on 20 July, at the Sea of Tranquillity. The two astronauts who landed—Edwin E. Aldrin, Jr, and Neil A. Armstrong—collected almost 50 pounds of lunar rock and set up many scientific experiments during their stay.

The Apollo 15 astronauts were the first 'motorists' on the moon: they used this electrically driven lunar rover to extend the range of their exploration. The umbrella-like device is an antenna.

The astronauts found that it was quite pleasant to walk on the moon, in spite of their heavy space suits and life-support equipment. The $\frac{1}{6}$ gravity of the moon allowed them to walk and even to lope at speeds up to 6 miles (9.7 kilometers) per hour without becoming very tired.

After $2\frac{1}{2}$ hours on the lunar surface, the astronauts returned to the lunar module. They lifted off, docked with the command module and returned to earth.

Five other landings on the moon were made. These were Apollo 12 (1969), Apollos 14 and 15 (1971) and Apollos 16 and 17 (1972). Each added to our store of information about the earth's only satellite. For example, the Apollo 17 astronauts gathered 250 pounds (113 kilograms) of rocks and soil, perhaps finding both the oldest and youngest lunar samples. Orange lunar soil, suggesting possible volcanic activity, was an unexpected discovery. The Apollo 17 astronauts stayed on the moon for 3 days—longer than any of the other astronauts.

FROM LIFT-OFF TO SPLASH-DOWN

A spacecraft that is to reach the moon must travel fast enough to overcome the earth's gravity. Gravity is the force that pulls objects towards the center of the earth. As an object gets further away, the pull of gravity weakens.

The speed needed to overcome gravity is called *escape velocity*. This speed is about 7 miles (11 kilometers) per second, or 25,000 miles (40,000 kilometers) per hour. Reaching escape velocity does not mean that the craft has freed itself completely of the earth's pull. But it does mean that it will not fall back to earth, even if no more power is used. The craft will continue its course away from the earth, until the gravity of the moon captures it.

A spacecraft can also travel at a lower speed that will put it into orbit round the earth. The craft then becomes a satellite of the earth. The speed needed to make this happen is called the *orbital velocity*.

The Launch

A spacecraft rides on top of its rocket engine. The Apollo spacecraft are launched by the Saturn V rocket. This enormous rocket has three separate parts, or stages, one mounted on top of another. Each stage carries its own fuel supply. The spacecraft sits on top of the third, or highest, stage. It is 36 storeys above the ground.

At launching time the first stage of the Saturn rocket fires. For a breathless second after ignition the rocket, weighing 3,000 tons, seems to stand motionless in a sea of flames. In the first 10 seconds it climbs only 300 feet (91.4 meters)—about its own length. But the engine is burning 15 tons of fuel every second, so that the Saturn is losing weight very quickly. Soon it is rising straight up, faster than a jet airliner flies. Only 2½ minutes after ignition, the first stage has burned all 2,200 tons of its fuel. It has pushed the whole rocket assembly to a height of 38 miles (58 kilometers) and a speed of 6,000 miles (9,600 kilometers) per hour. Its work done, the first stage drops away, tumbling into the ocean far below.

The spacecraft is freed of the enormous weight of the first stage and its fuel. Now the second stage fires. Its rockets push the assembly to still greater speeds. The second-stage rocket continues to burn for more than 6 minutes. By that time the rocket assembly is 115 miles (184 kilometers) above the earth and travelling at more than 15,000 miles (24,000 kilometers) per hour. As the spent second stage separates and tumbles earthwards, the third-stage rocket ignites.

Into Orbit

The third-stage rocket burns for 2½ minutes, bringing the craft up to orbital speed—17,500 miles (28,000 kilometers) per hour. The rocket fire shuts down, but the rocket and spacecraft remain attached as they go into an orbit round the earth. This orbit is known as a 'parking orbit'.

There are advantages in putting a spacecraft into a parking orbit before sending it further into space. First, it gives the astronauts a chance to check their instruments. Second, a craft launched directly into space would need more-powerful, more-expensive rockets. Scientists have also found that it is easier to aim a spacecraft towards its destination if the craft is first put into a parking orbit.

All Systems Go

A spaceship cannot simply be pointed towards its target, because the target is moving. An Apollo going to the moon must be aimed at a point in space where the moon will be when the trip ends 3 days later. There could be a difference of around 160,000 miles (256,000 kilometers) between these two points.

While the craft is in its parking orbit, computers constantly check and compare the positions of the earth, the moon and the spacecraft. All three are moving at different speeds in different directions. The computers must do millions of

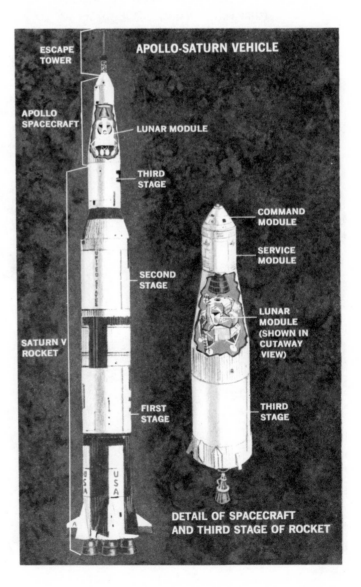

APOLLO-SATURN VEHICLE

ESCAPE TOWER

APOLLO SPACECRAFT

LUNAR MODULE

THIRD STAGE

SECOND STAGE

FIRST STAGE

SATURN V ROCKET

COMMAND MODULE

SERVICE MODULE

LUNAR MODULE (SHOWN IN CUTAWAY VIEW)

THIRD STAGE

DETAIL OF SPACECRAFT AND THIRD STAGE OF ROCKET

calculations to determine the exact course to the moon, the speed needed and the exact second that the rockets must be fired. At that exact second the third-stage engine starts again and burns for about 5 minutes. The push sends the craft out of earth orbit and into its long path towards the moon. Space scientists call this maneuver Trans-Lunar Injection, or TLI.

Space Jockeys

At lift-off the astronauts are at the top (that is, the front) of the spacecraft in the command module. Behind them is the service module, filled with machinery, tanks of fuel and oxygen and electrical equipment. Behind the service module is the lunar module, which will be used in the moon landing.

One thing the astronauts must do during their voyage from earth to the moon is move from the command module to the lunar module. There is no way to pass through the crowded service module so the crew must go through a maneuver called the 'turn-around'. The command and service modules (CSM), still attached to one another, pull away from the lunar module and slowly make a U-turn in

High above the earth, Apollo 9 astronaut David Scott leans out of the hatch of the command module. The photograph was taken by astronaut Russell Schweickart, who was in the docked lunar module.

space. The power to do this comes from a group of small rocket engines, called thrusters.

The CSM ease towards the LM until they are nose to nose. A tube-like probe passes between them and the two craft are locked together. Their nose sections now form a connecting tunnel through which the astronauts can move. With the modules firmly docked, the third stage is cast off. It drifts into space.

Keeping an Eye on Apollo

Where is the spacecraft? How fast is it travelling, and in what direction? The answers to these questions came from radar transmitters in tracking stations throughout the world. There are stations in Madrid, Spain, in Canberra, Australia, and in Goldstone, California. These sites were chosen so that at least one of the transmitters is in touch with the Apollo at any one time. Specially equipped ships and planes form the rest of the Apollo tracking system.

On the Moon

As the craft nears the moon it begins to speed up under the influence of the moon's gravity. If there were no way to slow it down, the spacecraft would crash on the moon's surface at a speed or more than 5,000 miles (8,000 kilometers) per hour. But the astronauts have a way to 'put on the brakes'. They turn the craft so that the rocket engine of the service module faces forwards, in the direction of flight. When the rocket is fired in this direction, it acts as a brake on the hurtling Apollo. A rocket used for slowing a spacecraft is called a *retro-rocket*. The Apollo slows to a speed of about 1,950 miles (3,120 kilometers) per hour and goes into orbit round the moon. The high point of the orbit is 190 miles (304 kilometers) above the moon, and the low point is 70 miles (112 kilometers). A second retro-rocket blast slows the craft again.

Now the lunar module must be prepared for the landing. Only two of the three astronauts make the trip down to the moon in the LM. The third man remains in the orbiting CSM. After the equipment and controls in the LM have been carefully checked, it is detached from the CM. For a short time the two craft fly together in orbit, only a few hundred yards apart. Then, at exactly the moment calculated by computers, the descent engine of the LM fires in the direction of flight. The craft loses speed. It begins a long, slanting fall towards the moon. The last stage of the moon landing begins about an hour later, when the LM is only 9 miles (15 kilometers) above the moon.

The firing of the descent engine is controlled by the computer. It orders the engine to start again, firing as a retro-rocket. The craft slows down and tilts gradually into a vertical position. A continuous stream of radar signals guides the computer, telling it how far away the moon's surface is and how fast the craft is descending.

The astronauts can take control of the craft away from the computer at any time they choose. At the very end of the landing they must do so, for the computer cannot pick out boulders and deep craters to be avoided.

Four long legs support the LM as it settles gently on the moon's surface. Landings can be made on slightly sloping hills, but too great a tilt could make the LM topple over. The lower part, or descent stage, of the LM must stand fairly straight. It will serve as the launching pad when the ascent stage, carrying the astronauts, blasts off from the moon.

Working On the Moon

The Apollo astronauts worked on several scientific problems while they were on the moon. They collected rocks and soil samples. Scientists hoped these samples could provide information about the history of the solar system. The astronauts also set up instruments that sent information back to earth about what was happening on the moon and in the space round it.

One of the instruments was a seismometer, which detects tremors (vibrations). Tremors on the moon's surface may be caused by moonquakes, volcanic eruptions and the impact of falling meteorites. The seismometer records the strength of the tremors, stores this information and on command radioes it to earth.

The astronauts also set up a device to measure the solar wind. The solar wind is a flow of electrified particles from the sun. Measurement of the speed and direction of the particles may help scientists learn more about the composition of the sun. These measurements are difficult to make on earth. This is because the earth has a strong magnetic field that changes the speed and direction of the electrified particles.

In another experiment the astronauts put a laser mirror in place on the moon. The mirror is made up of 100 reflectors of a special kind set in a frame. An intense laser beam was aimed at the moon from the earth. The beam stabbed through space like a pencil of light. It struck the laser mirror and was reflected. On earth, a powerful telescope detected the returning beam. This experiment enabled scientists to measure the distance between the earth and the moon to within one foot. The distance was calculated from the time it took the laser beam to reach the moon and return to earth. The accuracy of this measurement makes it possible to detect small variations in the orbits of the earth and moon.

Magnetometers that were put in place showed that the moon's magnetic field is less than $\frac{1}{100}$ as strong as that of the earth. Other instruments detected and measured the few particles of gas that might be called the moon's 'atmosphere'. The astronauts drilled holes into the moon's surface to obtain samples of the moon's deeper crust and to measure heat escaping from the moon. Most of the instruments were powered by small nuclear generators. Apollo 15, just before its return to earth, set free a sub-satellite that would remain in lunar orbit, sending back information about the moon's gravity and its magnetic field. Apollo 16 launched another sub-satellite.

THE JOURNEY HOME

Before lift-off the astronauts trigger a device that disconnects the ascent stage from the lower part of the LM. The men use radar in the LM to track the orbiting command-service module. They then set their automatic controls. The rocket engine fires at the right moment. The ascent stage rises straight up for a few seconds, then tilts to follow a course that will carry it up to meet the CSM in orbit. While both craft are moving near each other at almost the same speed, their nose sections are eased together to form a connecting tunnel. The moon explorers re-enter the CM through the tunnel. The LM is pushed away with a gentle rocket push. It will continue in orbit for a time, then crash on the moon.

Now the CSM must come out of its orbit round the moon. It is moving at 3,500 miles (5,600 kilometers) per hour. A burst of rocket fire adds another 3,300 miles (4,848 kilometers) per hour—

enough to break loose from the moon's gravity. This maneuver, called the Trans-Earth Injection (TEI), begins the long, coasting ride back to earth.

As the spacecraft nears the earth, the pull of gravity strengthens. It causes the craft to speed up. Towards the end of the homeward journey the craft is falling at nearly 25,000 miles (40,000 kilometers) per hour, about the same speed at which it left the earth.

Entering the Earth's Atmosphere

The rocket engine of the service module is fired for the last time. Its thrust sets the craft on a path called the re-entry corridor. The astronauts, in the CM, separate their craft from the SM. Following the re-entry corridor brings the CM into the earth's atmosphere at exactly the right slant. Too steep a slant would make the spacecraft bounce off the atmosphere and skip back into space.

Friction between the atmosphere and the walls of the capsule produces an enormous amount of heat. A few seconds after the capsule hits the atmosphere some parts of it glow white-hot with a temperature of 5000° C (9032° F). But the blunt end of the capsule is covered with a heat shield made of a special plastic. Before reaching the atmosphere, the astronauts turn the capsule so that the blunt end is facing forwards. As the heat increases, the plastic slowly melts and boils away. In this way the heat is kept away from the astronauts. Most of the heat shield is usually gone by the time the capsule lands.

Splash-Down

The resistance of the atmosphere slows the craft down suddenly. When the module is about 20,000 feet (6,100 meters) above the earth, small parachutes called *drogues* open. They steady the craft and slow it some more. At 10,000 feet (3,050 meters) much larger parachutes open. They lower the craft slowly down to the ocean. It floats there while the astronauts wait for helicopters to pick them up. Both the men and the module are flown to nearby ships.

LIVING ON THE MOON

Astronauts can live on the moon only if they carry with them oxygen to breathe. They must also be protected from radiation and the extreme temperatures on the moon. Space suits supply both oxygen and protection. But a space suit can be worn only for a short time. For periods of days or weeks on the moon, men would need the protection of buildings. Food and water would also be needed.

If there was ever water on the moon, it may still exist as ice at the bottom of some clefts. Sunlight would not have reached it there. Water is made up of hydrogen and oxygen. It can be separated into these gases with the help of electricity. Thus, it might be possible to provide oxygen for breathing and hydrogen for rocket fuel without bringing these gases from the earth. With water available, plants might be grown for food.

It may be possible some day to set up protected covered cities on the moon. The building materials and metals would be taken from the moon's rocks and soil. The necessary energy would come from sunlight. The sun's light and heat can be collected and focused by devices called solar furnaces. Sunlight can also be turned into electricity.

How the Moon Can Help Us

Cities on the moon may be far in the future, but scientific uses of the moon may come sooner. The moon is an ideal place for astronomical observatories. There is no atmosphere to interfere with observations. Telescopes on the moon could detect dimmer, more distant stars than is possible from the earth. Radio telescopes, which detect waves of radio energy from the stars, would be free from interference by the man-made radio waves on earth. Once an observatory is set up, men are not needed to run it. Automatic radio and television reporting to the earth is possible. Observatories on the moon may become a major tool for studying the universe.

The moon's surface may also be a key

to a better understanding of the earth's history. The rocks on the earth's surface have been melted and crushed by volcanic activity. Running water and winds have worn them away. As a result, there are no clues to what happened on the earth during the first billion or so years of its 4,500,000,000-year existence. On the moon there is no wind or running water, and perhaps no great volcanic activity. Scientists may find clues to the early history of our earth in the moon's rocks.

PROBING THE PLANETS

In 1969 Richard Nixon, then president of the United States, said that 'the journey of Apollo 11 to the moon and back was not an end but the beginning'. Within a few years of these words being spoken, American and Russian space probes were travelling to some of the earth's sister-planets.

The planets that have attracted the most attention are Mars and Venus. These are the planets that are closest to our own planet, Earth.

Mars is further away from the sun than the earth is. It circles the sun in an orbit that lies nearly 50,000,000 miles (80,000,000 kilometers) from the earth's orbit. Several probes have been sent to this 'red planet'. In fact, some space probes flew by the planet even before the first Apollo astronaut set foot on the moon.

In 1965 Mariner 4, an American spacecraft, flew past Mars and took the very first photographs of another planet. Mariners 6 and 7 also took photographs of Mars. But the most successful Mars probe was Mariner 9. It reached Mars in November 1971 after a 167-day flight. It then became the first man-made satellite to go into orbit round another planet. The cameras on Mariner 9 operated for

A photograph of Mars taken by Mariner 9 from a distance of 445,000 miles (716,000 kilometers).

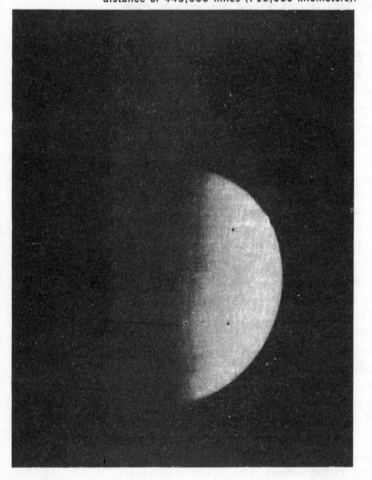

11 months, mapping the entire surface of that planet.

The Russians have also sent space probes to Mars, though with less success than the Americans. Mars 3 was launched in 1971; it returned scientific data about the planet for 3 months. In the summer of 1973, the Russians launched four more Mars probes, but two of these failed.

Venus is closer to the sun than the earth is, and it is the planet nearest to the earth. Both the Russians and the Americans have sent probes to investigate the Venusian atmosphere and surface.

Mariners 2 and 5, launched in the 1960s, flew past Venus before going into solar orbit. But it was the Russian probes, Venera 7 and Venera 8, that first sent back important information about Venus. They measured the planet's surface temperature and atmospheric pressure. It was discovered that Venus has a very hot atmosphere, and that 97 per cent of the atmosphere is carbon dioxide. The Venera 8 probe also detected uranium, potassium and thorium on the Venusian surface.

The third planet to be photographed was Mercury, the planet that is closest to the sun. In March 1974 the American Mariner 10 flew past Mercury. It sent back

A scale model of the Viking probe. Part of the craft is designed to land on Mars, while the other part continues in orbit. The probe will carry cameras, and instruments to measure temperature and atmospheric pressure.

Pioneer 10 begins its journey to Jupiter. It passed the planet in December 1973.

meters) and took more than 600 photographs. Mercury's magnetic field was also measured by the Mariner 10 probes. Until Mariner 10 visited Mercury, little was known about the planet. Astronomers have found it difficult to study because it is so near the sun.

Perhaps the most successful—and fascinating—of the planetary probes were Pioneer 10 and Pioneer 11. Launched in the same year as Mariner 10, the Pioneers were set to travel outwards to the planet Jupiter and beyond. They travelled further from the sun than any man-made object has ever done. Pioneer 10 spent 21 months covering the 620,000,000 miles (1,000,000,000 kilometers) of space between the earth and Jupiter, the largest of the sun's planets.

Pioneer 10 flew within 81,000 miles (130,000 kilometers) of Jupiter. It sent back dazzling color photographs and volumes of scientific data. The photographs showed Jupiter's brilliant bands, caused by gases flowing at different speeds, and its unexplained Red Spot, which is some 30,000 miles (48,000 kilometers) long.

After photographing Jupiter, Pioneer 10 continued its journey through space. By 1980 Pioneer 10 will become the first spacecraft ever to leave the solar system.

In December 1974 Pioneer 11 also flew past Jupiter. It passed through Jupiter's inner radiation belt and then took photographs of the Jovian poles. It also measured the heat in the Jovian atmosphere, and investigated Callisto, one of Jupiter's moons. Some space scientists believe that this moon could perhaps be used as a base from which astronauts will venture even further into space.

In 1979, just before Pioneer 10 leaves the solar system, Pioneer 11 will perhaps travel to Saturn.

photographs which show that Mercury's surface is full of craters. The probe also confirmed that this very hot planet has an atmosphere.

In September 1974, Mariner 10 paid a second visit to Mercury, and in March 1975 it passed by that planet for the third and last time. On this visit it soared past at an altitude of 198 miles (319 kilo-

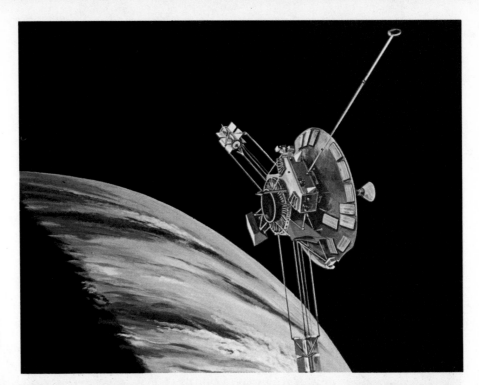

Right: An artist's conception of how Pioneer 10 appeared as it orbited Jupiter. Below: A photo of Jupiter taken by Pioneer 10 shows the Red Spot, the shadow of one of its moons, and atmospheric bands.

Venus—Our Nearest Planetary Neighbor

Venus is the second planet from the sun. After the sun and the moon, it appears as the brightest object in the sky. It is especially visible at dawn and at dusk. The orbit of Venus is between those of Mercury and Earth. In fact, every 584 days the Earth and Venus are closer to one another than any other planets in the solar system.

Although Venus is our nearest planetary neighbor—both in size and position—it remained a mystery. Because the planet is veiled by a thick blanket of

An artist's rendition of multiprobe Pioneer-Venus 2 shows the Bus entering Venus' atmosphere and taking measurements before it burns up. Smaller probes head toward their targets while Pioneer-Venus 1 remains in orbit above.

MISSIONS PROFILE

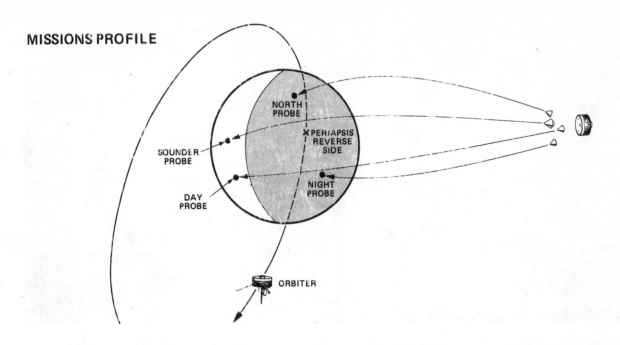

clouds, its surface cannot be seen from Earth, even with the aid of the strongest telescope.

The development of radio astronomy, which uses radio waves instead of light, enabled scientists to study the surface of Venus for the first time. In 1956, American astronomers found that the surface temperatures of Venus were hot enough to melt lead.

In the early 1960s, radar and microwave signals sent to Venus and returned to Earth discovered that Venus' daytime and nighttime temperatures were the same. The dense clouds which form Venus' atmosphere trap the sun's rays and keep the surface hot at all times.

SPACE VOYAGES TO VENUS

The first successful close look at Venus came from Mariner 2 in 1962. In 1967 America's Mariner 5 and the Soviet Venera 4 approached Venus. Venera 4 parachuted an instrument package toward Venus' surface. It transmitted data for 75 minutes and recorded temperatures of up to 267°C (513°F). It ceased transmission while it was still 20 miles (30 kilometers) above the surface.

Mariner 5 undertook a fly-by of Venus' day and night sides. It discovered that the atmosphere of Venus, which is nearly all carbon dioxide, is about 100 times as dense as the Earth's at sea level.

The Pioneer-Venus probes in 1978 were the most dramatic missions to Venus. Pioneer-Venus 1 went into Venusian orbit and sent atmospheric data back to Earth. Pioneer-Venus 2 was the mother ship for four probes that detached and entered the atmosphere to survey the planet's weather, chemistry and geology.

The Sounder Probe studied Venus' lower atmosphere, measuring clouds and atmospheric composition. A pod called the Bus contained three smaller probes which entered the atmosphere at different points. These probes gathered data on the circulation of the lower atmosphere, while the Bus measured the upper atmosphere. The information gathered by these probes solved some of the mysteries of Venus.

Mars—Where There Are Signs of Life

This computer-enhanced Martian sunset over Chryse Planitia was taken a month after Viking 1 landed. Shortly after sunset, the Martian surface seems almost black. The blue to red color variation of the sky is caused by the effects of the thin Martian atmosphere on the sun's rays. The portion of the horizon that is nearest the sun's position appears white because the bright rays saturated the camera.

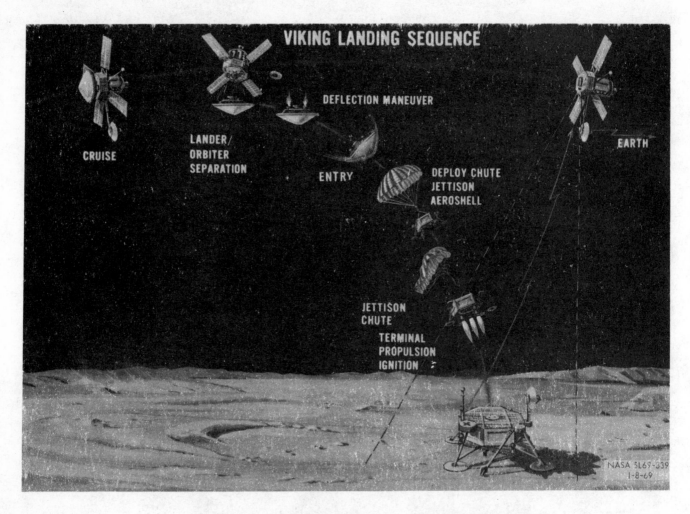

The Viking Lander separates from the windmill-like Orbiter. A parachute opened to slow its fall to Mars. As it approached the surface, the chute was discarded and the Lander's engines slowed its final approach.

Mars is the fourth planet from the sun. It is somewhat larger than half the size of Earth. The Martian day is nearly the same as the Earth's—24 hours and 37 minutes—but it has a 687-day year. Mars has an atmosphere but it is very thin. Two small, fast-orbiting moons, Deimos and Phobos, revolve around the planet.

The planet Mars has been observed for thousands of years. Ancient peoples identified this planet with their gods of war because Mars' reddish color reminded them of the ferocity of battle. The name *Mars* is in fact Roman.

The continuing development of the science of astronomy and improved telescopes have given many scientists hope that life existed on Mars. Observers discovered white polar caps, an atmosphere with clouds, and changing patterns of light and dark that could indicate vegetation. Telescopes also revealed a web of lines which some people theorized might be canals dug by intelligent beings.

LOOKING AT MARS FROM SPACE

Observations of Mars made from space, first begun in the 1960s, disproved

The Lander is 5 feet (1.5 meters) across and 1.5 feet (.5 meter) high. It is stabilized by adjustable feet. Its footpads contain sensing instruments. Cameras are housed in the two tall cylinders. The dish on the top is a powerful antenna.

some of these ideas. It was not until a spacecraft landed on Mars that a true picture of its curious surface developed.

The United States' Mariner space probes provided the first close look at the Red Planet. The 22 pictures transmitted in 1964 by Mariner 4 were followed by those sent by Mariners 6 and 7.

In 1971 Mariner 9 was launched to orbit Mars. By the time transmissions ended in November, 1972, scientists had a collection of 7,300 photographs covering all of the Martian surface.

Two Viking spacecraft were launched toward Mars in 1975. Each took about a year to reach its destination. The landing of Viking 1 had been planned for late June, 1976 but close-up photos showed that the area which had been chosen was scarred by deep cracks and vast upheavals. Hundreds of photos were studied to find a more suitable landing site.

While Viking 1 was in a holding pattern in orbit above Mars, Viking 2 was racing toward the planet for a planned September landing. Scientists wanted Viking 1 on the Martian ground before Viking 2 landed.

Finally, scientists located a flat section on a vast plain known as Chryse Planitia. Mission planners knew that the landing would still be difficult. The relative positions of Earth and Mars on July 20, the rescheduled landing date, made communications difficult. It would take about 20 minutes for data from Viking 1 to reach Earth. It would also take 20 minutes for commands from Earth to be relayed to Viking 1. This delay meant that there would be no chance for correction once Viking 1 had been commanded to commence the landing sequence.

The Viking spacecraft had two parts— the *Orbiter* and the *Lander*. The Orbiter was designed to remain in orbit around Mars and the Lander to collect data from the Martian surface and relay it to Earth.

Shortly after midnight on July 20 mission control signaled the Lander to separate from the Orbiter and begin its descent to the Martian surface. The landing process began with a half-hour engine burn to release the Lander from orbit. The Lander then parachuted to the Martian surface. Within an hour after landing Viking 1 was sending black-and-white pictures of the Martian landscape back to Earth. The following day it started transmitting color pictures.

ROCKY, RUSTY MARS

The pictures of Mars showed a rust-colored landscape strewn with rocks and overlaid with a film of fine dust. Mars' russet appearance was enhanced by the dust, which hung in the atmosphere like haze.

Viking's cameras focused on thousands of rocks. Geologists quickly identified more than 30 different kinds of rocks but many could not be categorized because

they were different from those on Earth.

The Lander's instruments measured a harsh environment. The atmosphere was about 95 per cent carbon dioxide. Temperatures during daylight hours ranged from $-123°F$ ($-86°C$) to a mid-afternoon high of $-24°F$ ($-31°C$). But the 3 per cent nitrogen content in the atmosphere meant that Martian life may once have existed.

Even more exciting than nitrogen, which is considered necessary to sustain life, was evidence that Mars had once been a watery planet. The Martian polar caps were found to be composed of water ice. Through the eyes of Viking 1's cameras, scientists were able to watch ice fogs form in Martian craters. Other data suggested that water was also locked in the ground in the form of permafrost.

The Lander was also equipped with a scoop and three miniaturized laboratories for collecting and analyzing soil samples. Biologists were already satisfied that the nitrogen, water and sunlight found on Mars could indicate the presence of primitive life such as bacteria. But another series of experiments began to test for the presence of the element carbon. For biologists, carbon is another indicator of life as we know it on Earth.

The first in a series of tests was the *gas exchange* experiment. In this test, soil is humidified and instruments measure changes in certain gases important in biology. This experiment showed that a large burst of oxygen was released from the soil as soon as it was humidified. Scientists were not sure whether this was a chemical reaction unknown on Earth or a biological clue to life.

The second test was the *labeled release* experiment. It looked for the release of carbon dioxide, like that released by animals on Earth when turning food into en-

A camera aboard Viking 1 took this photograph of the Lander and the rocky landscape of Chryse Planitia. Geologists have identified over 30 different types of rocks from such pictures. The dish-shaped object at the top is the Lander's antenna.

ergy. To conduct this experiment a sample of martian soil was "fed" with seven simple organic foods. These foods were radioactive so that any discharge could be measured. Radioactive carbon dioxide was produced by the soil sample.

The third test exposed a soil sample to carbon dioxide, carbon monoxide and simulated sunlight. Martian organisms, if they existed, would turn these carbon gases into organic substances. Organic substances were produced by the first soil sample. When the experiment was repeated with a soil sample that had been sterilized, no organic substances were produced. To scientists this result meant that microbes present in the Martian soil might have been killed during the sterilization process.

No organic substances were found in the Martian soil samples, so scientists were not ready to say that life had been

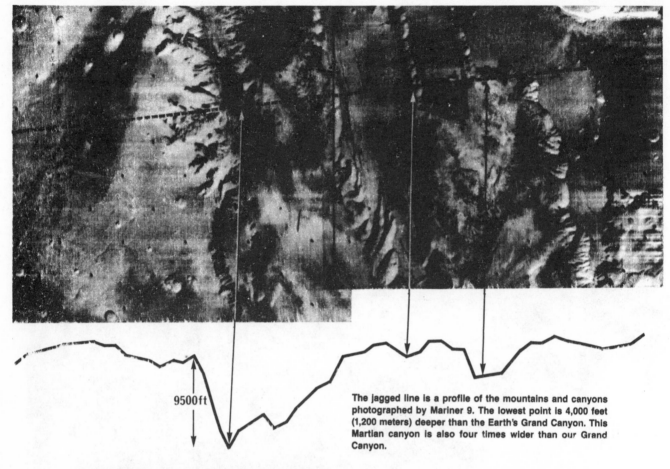

9500 ft

The jagged line is a profile of the mountains and canyons photographed by Mariner 9. The lowest point is 4,000 feet (1,200 meters) deeper than the Earth's Grand Canyon. This Martian canyon is also four times wider than our Grand Canyon.

Viking 1's Orbiter photographed the canyon, named Valles Marineris, through violet, green and red filters to produce this mosaic. Valles Marineris is just south of the Martian equator. North is toward the upper left.

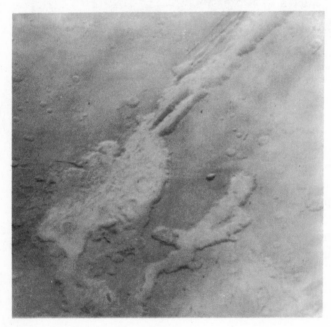

found on Mars. But no one was ready to dismiss the possibility.

THE QUEST CONTINUES

Viking 2 landed on September 3, 1976 in a more northern region of Mars called Utopia.

Viking 2's signals showed more water at Utopia than Chryse Planitia. Although the view from Viking 2's Lander looked similar to the Mars-scape around Viking 1, the second Lander found an unusual pattern of connected troughs.

The Future of the Viking Mission

Both Viking Landers are powered by long-lasting nuclear sources and both Viking Orbiters are solar-powered. During the life-span of these missions, data continues to return to Earth regarding the nature of the universe and the Red Planet Mars.

To Jupiter—The Giant of Our Solar System

Jupiter is the giant among the planets which orbit our sun. It is 11 times the diameter of the Earth. Huge Jupiter was named after the king of the Roman gods.

Jupiter travels in companionship with 13 moons. The four largest, which were discovered by the astronomer Galileo in 1609, are each larger than our own moon. They can even be seen with powerful field glasses. Jupiter is the first of the outer planets, whose orbits are separated from those of Mercury, Venus, Earth and Mars by a belt of interplanetary debris called asteroids.

Astronomers have long trained their telescopes on this giant of the solar system. They knew that Jupiter has very long years and very short days. A Jupiter, or

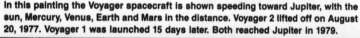

In this painting the Voyager spacecraft is shown speeding toward Jupiter, with the sun, Mercury, Venus, Earth and Mars in the distance. Voyager 2 lifted off on August 20, 1977. Voyager 1 was launched 15 days later. Both reached Jupiter in 1979.

Voyager 1 photographed Jupiter from a distance of 25 million miles (40,000,000 kilometers). The satellite Ganymede is at the lower left.

Great Red Spot changes in intensity, color and size.

PIONEER FINDINGS

Four unmanned U.S. spacecraft have flown past Jupiter and sent data back to Earth. But each mission raised as many questions as it answered. Pioneer 10, which was launched in 1972, was the first probe sent to the outer planets. It passed Jupiter nine months after its launch. Four weeks later it crossed the orbit of Hades, Jupiter's outermost moon.

Pioneer 11 lifted off later that year. Its first mission was to collect data on the vast interplanetary space between Mars and Jupiter. After it had passed the asteroid belt between the two planets it continued the research on Jupiter begun by Pioneer 10.

Pioneer 10 made many important dis-

This painting shows Voyager's instruments aimed at Jupiter. Voyager monitored the planet and five of its moons.

Jovian, year is equal to almost 12 Earth years. But a day on Jupiter is less than 10 hours long. Because of the planet's rapid rotation, Jupiter is flattened out slightly at the poles and bulges at the equator.

Jupiter does not have a crust of rock as the four inner planets do. Pioneers 10 and 11, which flew past Jupiter in the mid-1970s, confirmed that the planet is a spinning globe of liquid hydrogen. Telescopes show striped markings which run parallel to the equator. These seem to be bands of rising and descending gas.

In addition to these bands, Jupiter shows streaks, wisps, arches, plumes and spots which seem to be clouds whipping stormily through the atmosphere. Jupiter's most famous surface feature is a huge red spot in the southern hemisphere. This

coveries about Jupiter's magnetic field. Like the Earth, Jupiter is protected from solar winds by an invisible magnetic field called the magnetosphere. Unlike the Earth's, Jupiter's magnetosphere is oddly shaped. Particles spin out from the magnetosphere, drawing the field with them. This energy and the pull of Jupiter's larger moons distort the magnetosphere.

The Pioneer program has also increased our knowledge of Jupiter's interior and its weather. Scientists now know that Jupiter is a huge spinning ball without any apparent solid surface. It is composed mostly of liquid hydrogen. Helium, ammonia and methane have also been found in the Jovian atmosphere. There is no sharp line separating the surface from the atmosphere. There is a gradual transition from liquid to gas between the surface and the atmosphere.

Voyager 1 photographed the Great Red spot through a violet filter. Clouds as small as 100 miles (160 kilometers) are visible.

Jupiter's Great Red Spot was the target of spacecraft investigations. This is an artist's idea of how Pioneer looked over it.

Compared to the inner planets, which are closer to the sun, Jupiter is very cold. Surface temperatures are more than 200°F below zero (-129°C). But scientists speculate that its interior temperature must be 26,000°F (14,430°C). In fact, Jupiter radiates more heat than it absorbs from the far-away sun.

Jupiter's atmosphere is full of constantly-moving clouds. They are probably made of ammonia and ammonium compounds. They form by condensation, just as the Earth's clouds do.

Pioneer's measurements led scientists to conclude that the planet's belt-like markings are hurricanes. Compared to storms on Earth, these are large and violent because the forces causing them emerge from the planet's interior.

THE LONG TRIP OF VOYAGER

In August and September of 1977, two 1,800-pound (818-kilogram) Voyager spacecraft lifted off for Jupiter and beyond. The mission will take nine years to reach the outer solar system.

The main purpose of the mission is to explore Jupiter and its 13 moons and later compare it with Saturn and its 10 moons and famous rings. Each spacecraft is packed with identical instruments. The most noticeable feature of the Voyager is the huge saucer-shaped antenna which is used to relay data back to Earth. This data is collected by two television cameras and other instruments. Voyagers' routes are different, and the dates when they encounter the planets are different too.

Voyagers travel faster than any previous spacecraft. It took Apollo astronauts three days to get to the moon. Voyager passed the moon's orbit only 10 hours after liftoff. Eighty days before the closest approach to Jupiter, the instruments began observing the giant planet. Voyager 1's closest approach to Jupiter was a quarter of a million miles. At this point, the instruments were in the best position to study the planet's atmosphere and its closest large moon, Io.

When Voyager 1 was 12.5 million miles (20 million kilometers) from Jupiter, it took this photo of the planet and its moons Io (left), and Europa. Scientists believe Io is composed of a mixture of salts and sulfur. Its mottled appearance contrasts with Europa. Although both satellites have about the same brightness, Io's color is very different from Europa's.

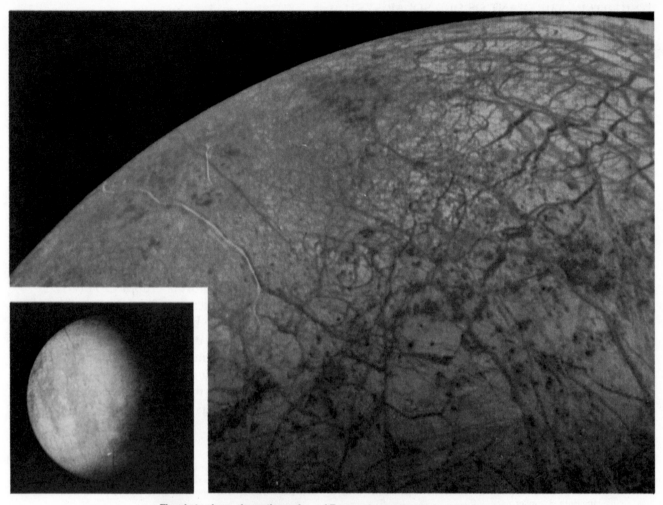

The photo above shows the surface of Europa, the smallest of Jupiter's four major moons. Scientists believe the icy surface is covered with cracks. The inset shows a Voyager 2 photo of a 12-mile (20-kilometer) detail. Below (left) is Ganymede, Jupiter's largest moon, as photographed by Voyager 2. The bright spots are craters. Below (right) is a close-up of Ganymede.

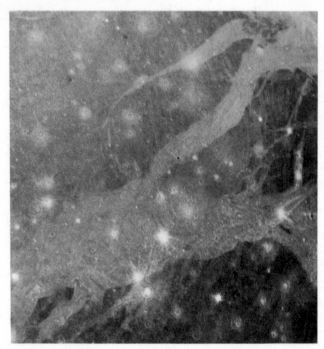

Voyager 2 took this picture of Jupiter on June 10, 1979 showing the shadow of Ganymede on top of the brightly colored cloud patterns. Io, the innermost of the major moons, is to the right of Jupiter.

Voyager 2's flight path took it close to Jupiter's small innermost moon, Amalthea, and the three other large moons, Europa, Callisto and Ganymede.

Both Voyagers kept their appointments with Jupiter in 1979. They sent back exciting pictures. First, Voyager 1 discovered a ring system which even the Pioneer flybys had not detected. Voyager 2 cameras photographed these rings from above and below. These rings of debris circle Jupiter's equator about 35,000 miles (58,300 kilometers) above the cloud tops.

Voyager 2 also took close-ups of the Great Red Spot. Scientists now know that the atmosphere above this red spot rotates. They also know that the lower levels rotate faster than the upper ones. This makes it seem that the Great Red Spot's rotation begins deep in the interior of Jupiter.

Voyager also gave astronomers the first close look at Jupiter's major satellites. Callisto appears to have a relatively smooth surface. Ganymede's surface is full of cracks and gorges. Europa's surface is covered by veins that may be crevices in an icy sea. The greatest surprise came from Io. Voyager 1 photographed eight volcanoes in the midst of erupting. This is the first time volcanoes have been discovered anywhere but on Earth.

Following the outstanding developments from the encounter with Jupiter, Voyager 2 was sent further out into space. It is scheduled to monitor Saturn in August, 1981 and distant Uranus in January, 1986.

This is an artist's conception of Voyager 1 as it passes through the "flux tube," a region of magnetic phenomenon between the satellite Io (upper right) and Jupiter (lower left).

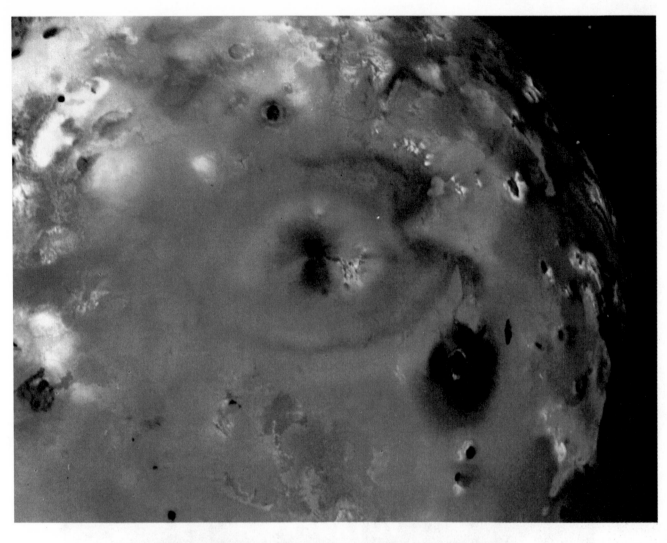

Voyager 1 took the above photo of Io from a distance of 226,200 miles (377,000 kilometers). Many of the black spots are probably volcanic craters. The photos below show volcanic action on Io. The bright blue may be volcanic gases and the dark areas in the volcanoes may be molten sulfur.

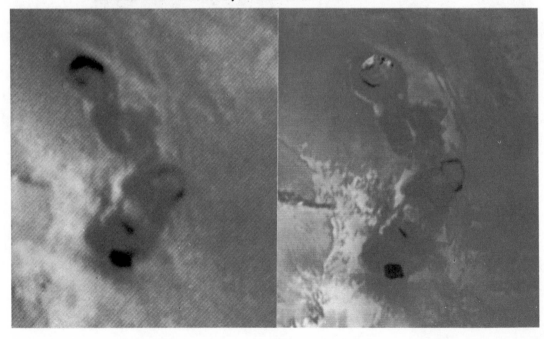

Next Stop: Saturn

Many astronomers believe that Saturn is the most beautiful planet in the solar system—a globe circled by glowing rings. Even before spacecraft were launched to explore the solar system, astronomers knew that these rings, which were discovered long ago, are made of ice crystals.

Saturn is Jupiter's nearest planetary neighbor and the two have many similarities. Saturn is the second largest planet in the solar system—only Jupiter is larger. Saturn has 10 moons. Only Jupiter, with 13 moons, has more satellites. Both planets are fast spinning and have an atmosphere composed largely of hydrogen and helium. The bands seen on the surface

The two Voyager spacecraft were launched from Earth to explore the outer planets, as shown in this drawing. After their successful exploration of Jupiter, they continued to Saturn. Voyager 2 will reach Uranus after a 7-year flight.

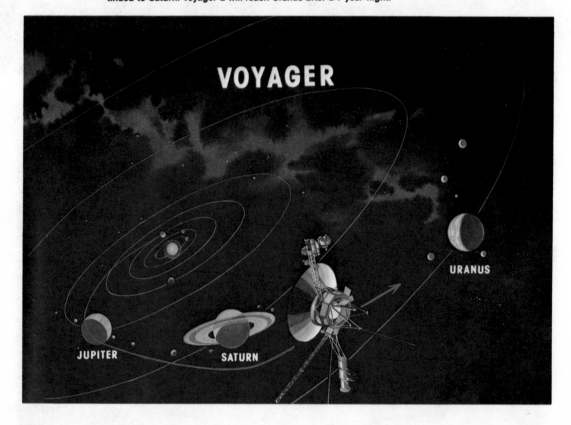

A Voyager probe is painted here as it approaches Saturn and its rings. The dish-like antenna signals findings back to Earth. The arms projecting from the craft contain cameras and other instruments.

of Saturn and Jupiter are formed by clouds. Like Jupiter, Saturn gives off more heat than it absorbs from the sun. Saturn's surface temperature of about 300°F below zero (-184°C) is warmer than expected. As with Jupiter, scientists believe that the interior of Saturn must be very hot.

Saturn is the least dense planet. In fact, Saturn is less dense than water. If there were an ocean large enough to hold a massive planet, Saturn would float. All the other planets would sink.

The second largest moon in the solar system is Saturn's Titan. It is as large as the planet Mercury. As far as astronomers know, Titan is the only moon in the solar system with its own atmosphere. They think that the atmosphere of Titan might even be as dense as that found on Earth.

Unlike Jupiter, Saturn sends out no natural radio waves. Perhaps Saturn has a strong magnetic field. Maybe it has no source of electrons to send off in the form of radio waves. Or perhaps the rings somehow interfere with such signals.

The two Voyager spacecraft that lifted off in 1977 are scheduled to fly by Saturn in 1981. The volumes of data they relay back to Earth will have to be sorted out and analyzed before scientists come up with some of the answers to the puzzle of the outer planets.

The next step for exploring Saturn would be to launch an orbiter that would send back data over a longer period of time. Mission experts have already calculated that the best time to launch a man-made Saturn satellite would be in 1985.

Space Shuttle—The Next Step

Engineers and scientists have accomplished modern miracles since the first Pioneer probe was launched into space in 1958. Scores of satellites have been put into orbit around the Earth. Men have walked in space and on the moon. Spacecraft equipped with sensitive instruments have been launched into space to send back information that will help explain some of the mysteries of our solar system.

The huge center tube of the Space Shuttle is the fuel tank, which will be discarded.
The smaller side tubes are the reusable booster rockets.

(Above) A 747 jet plane served as a "launching pad" for early Space Shuttle tests. The first flights carried the unmanned vehicle for a ride in the atmosphere. (Below) Manned rides atop the 747 taxi were the second step. In eight manned "free flights" the unpowered Shuttle will simulate the glide back to Earth.

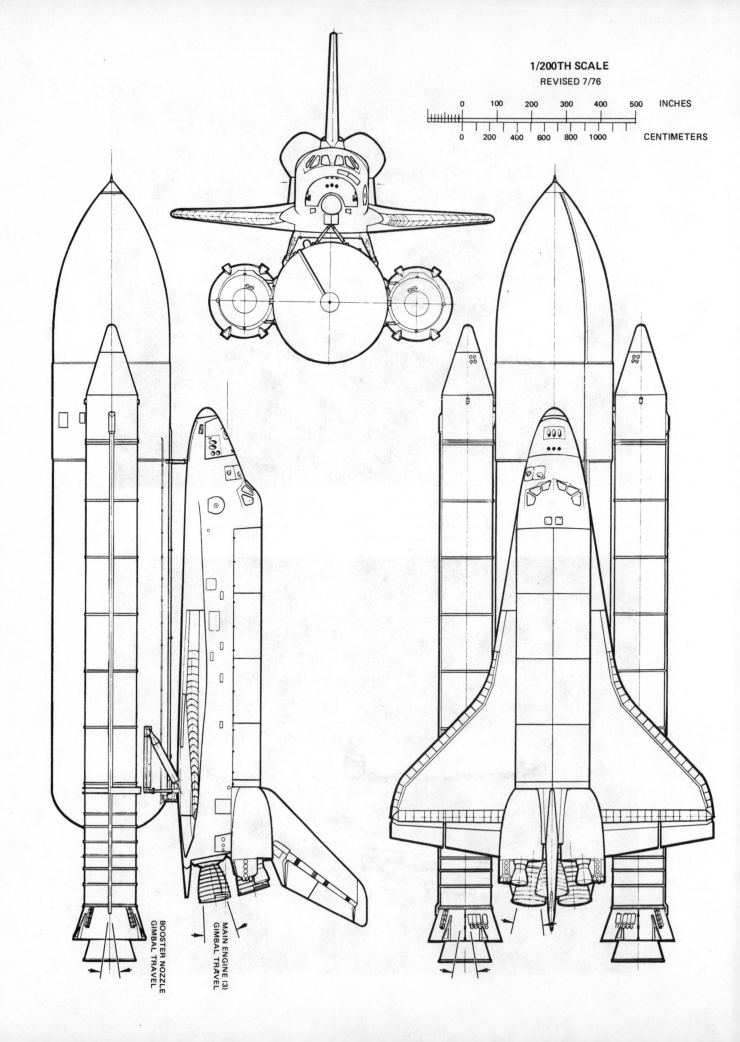

1/200TH SCALE
REVISED 7/76

0   100   200   300   400   500   INCHES

0   200   400   600   800   1000   CENTIMETERS

BOOSTER NOZZLE
GIMBAL TRAVEL

MAIN ENGINE (3)
GIMBAL TRAVEL

(Above) The Shuttle is loaded for flight. (Below) Observation equipment is an important part of the craft. (Bottom) The Space Shuttle will be used to service satellites in orbit. Since the vehicle can be reused often, it will be relatively inexpensive to operate.

All of these programs have had one thing in common. They were wasteful. Every spacecraft that was launched into space resulted in the loss of millions of dollars worth of equipment. Only capsules were recovered and they were not reused.

The first project to break this pattern was the Space Shuttle. This ambitious program offered the first real cost breakthrough in space exploration.

WHAT IS THE SPACE SHUTTLE?

The Space Shuttle is a cross between a regular aircraft and a space vehicle. It is about the size and shape of a DC-9 airplane and can carry instruments and a crew of seven astronauts. The astronauts will live in a three-level cabin at the nose of the craft. The fuselage contains compartments outfitted as laboratories and cargo areas.

In tests conducted in 1978, the Shuttle was carried piggyback style high into the atmosphere on the top of a 747 airplane. Future Shuttles will take off vertically from a launching pad with the aid of two powerful booster rockets. These expensive rockets, which push the craft out of the atmosphere, will parachute back to Earth so that they may be used again.

Once in orbit, the Space Shuttle will maneuver like a spacecraft. The Shuttle is designed to glide back through the atmosphere and land like an airplane.

After the Space Shuttle has returned from a mission, it can be resupplied for another journey into space. Planners say that a single vehicle will be capable of making a hundred space flights.

How the Shuttle Works

The Shuttle will be the American workhorse of space. It will be used to inspect and repair unmanned satellites in or-

The Space Shuttle is shown ready for vertical takeoff. The two booster rockets will burn enough fuel to carry the vehicle high above the Earth before it continues under its own power. The huge fuel tank will burn up as it falls through the atmosphere and the boosters will parachute into the sea for recovery.

bit. The craft will even be able to bring satellites back to Earth for repairs that cannot be done by astronauts in space.

The Space Shuttle will also be able to place parts of interplanetary craft into orbit around the Earth so that they can be checked and assembled before being sent into space.

One of the most important tools for astronomers will be the Sky Telescope. It will monitor the universe without atmospheric interference. The Shuttle and its crew will be able to orbit, set up, service and return these telescopes to Earth.

A NEW ROLE FOR PEOPLE

The astronauts who will live and work in the early Space Shuttles will be different from the astronauts of the past. The people who were trained for the Earth-orbiting and moon programs were, for the most part, military men, pilots, and scientists. One of the most exciting aspects of the Space Shuttle program is that it offers everyone a chance to qualify. The new crop of astronauts will include women as well as more civilian scientists.

The first piggyback Shuttle flights have already taken place. The first independent orbiting flight is scheduled for 1980. The ship will orbit the Earth every 90 minutes, cruising at a speed of 17,000 miles (28,300 kilometers) an hour. This flight will usher in a new era for all people, expanding their world into outer space.

The Future—
Living in Space

Every manned spaceflight launched by the United States and the Soviet Union has been another step toward the colonization of space. This is a goal that has been envisioned by science fiction writers and dreamed about by scientists for ages.

American astronauts lived and worked aboard Skylab for 84 days in 1973-74. Soviet cosmonauts spent a record 175 days aboard a Soyuz spacecraft in 1979. Amer-

An artist has painted a wheel-shaped space colony rotating in space. In this view the habitat is shown reflected in an astronaut's helmet.

ican and Russian space travelers even showed that cooperation in space is possible by the successful linkup of Apollo and Soyuz spacecraft in 1975.

These programs have taught scientists a great deal about what it takes for people to live and work together in space. But comparing even the largest manned spacecraft of the past with space colonies of the future is like comparing a rowboat to an ocean liner. Scientists foresee communities in space populated by thousands of people.

Space colonies are not really a new idea. Edward Everett Hale wrote a novel in 1869 called *Brick Moon*. In this story, a brick sphere was going to be sent into space by spinning wheels. The sphere accidentally rolled onto the catapult while there were workmen aboard and it was sent flying into space. The workers had plenty of food with them, so they decided to live in space and communicate with Earth by Morse Code.

Motion pictures have also contributed to the number of fantasies about outer space. Films such as *2001: A Space Odyssey* and *Star Wars* took place on colonies rush-

This illustration, like all that follow, is an artist's depiction of a design for a space colony. The wheel-shaped habitat would house 10,000 people. People can live and work in space only if they are protected from radioactivity and other harmful rays by a shield. The docking area is in the center of the hub.

ing through deep space. These films gave movie-goers an idea of what huge space colonies might look like.

MAKING PLANS

Scientists and engineers have produced mathematical formulas, diagrams and drawings for space colonies. They have based their plans on their own ideas and what space probes have taught them. They have thought about power sources, food, elimination of waste, recreation, weightlessness and thousands of other things that are all part of living in space.

But if a space colony is to be successful, scientists believe that it must be self-supporting and productive. Solar energy and materials gathered from the moon would be used by space colonists. Solar power would heat furnaces which in turn would refine materials taken from the moon. Eventually, satellite solar power stations and new colonies would be built in space from ores mined on the moon.

NASA designers have planned a space colony that looks like a giant wheel. The outer rim of this wheel consists of a 427-foot-wide (129-meter) tube that is bent

The giant wheel floats through space. The central hub contains the docking station and communications antenna. Six spokes connect the hub with the living and working spaces in the "tire" portion of the wheel. To simulate Earth's gravity, the entire space habitat rotates once per minute.

into the shape of a ring. People would live in the ring-shaped tube. This tube would be connected to a central hub by six access routes that look like the spokes of a wheel. Spaceships would use the central hub of the ring as a docking area.

The space habitat would travel around the sun in a small orbit of its own. Scientists have plotted five possible orbits which would be in balance with the gravity of the Earth and the moon.

In this imaginary habitat, natural sunlight would bounce off a mirror and light the interior. The colony would be exposed to sunlight but protected from harmful radiation. Farming would take place within the colony with the help of natural sunshine. Because of the abundance of sunlight, scientists believe that enough

This detail of the hub shows the docking facilities, antenna and access spokes to the living area. The webbed material between the spokes is the colony's solar power cells.

A cross-section shows how the interior of the wheel might look. The chevron-shaped shields at the top are mirrors that reflect light into the colony while screening out harmful rays.

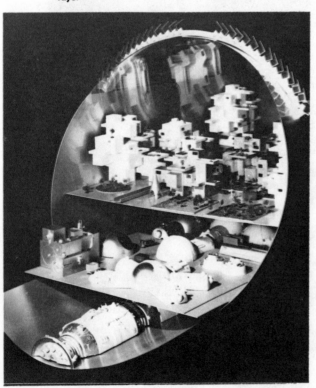

food could be raised on one colony to feed 10,000 people.

WEIGHTLESSNESS

One of the main problems facing human beings who live in space is the condition of weightlessness. Being completely free from gravity is a very strange sensation. On Earth, everyone is constantly affected by gravity. It shows us what is up and what is down. It makes some objects heavy and other objects light. It keeps things resting on the ground or on horizontal surfaces.

Manned spaceflights have taught scientists how the body reacts to long periods of weightlessness. When astronauts return to the Earth's gravitational influence, they feel weak and tire easily until their bodies

A space colony can become a world whirling through outer space. Constructed mostly of ore mined from the moon, the interior of this habitat would have all the comforts of an Earthly home—trees, parks, birds, grass, streams and ponds. It would also have functional buildings in which to live and work. The chevron-shaped mirrors overhead let in limitless sunlight.

readjust to being on Earth again.

Scientists have found that human bones lose calcium at the rate of 1 to 2 per cent per month of weightlessness. This means that bone fractures from even minor bumps are a real danger after a long period in space.

In order to counteract such problems, space colonies must be designed to produce artificial gravity. Rapid rotation of the entire habitat would create a force resembling gravity on Earth.

One real benefit of weightlessness is that it would make supermen, superwomen and even superkids of everyone. Because things in space have no weight,

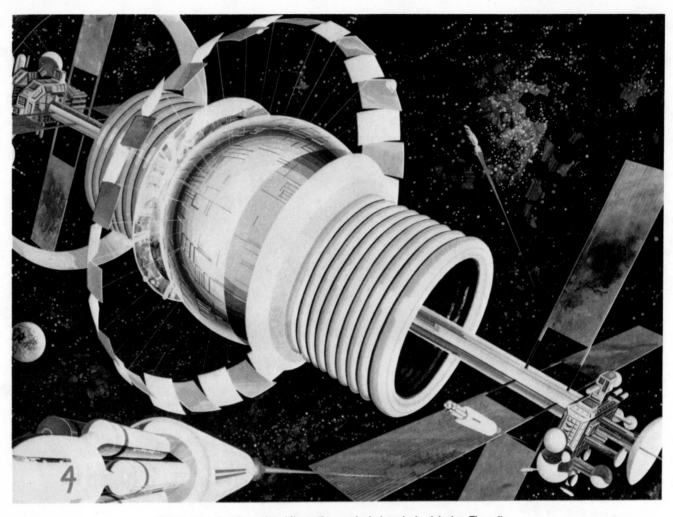

This space colony is an alternative to the popular hub-and-wheel design. The cylindrical colony rotates to mimic Earth's gravity, but it contains zero-gravity docking areas with industrial zones at each end. The band of flat plates is designed to bounce waste heat away from the habitat and into space.

human beings would be able to perform tasks that are impossible on Earth.

Future space colonies will have to be designed to take advantage of the benefits of weightlessness while avoiding the harm it can do to people.

HELPING PEOPLE ADJUST TO SPACE

We do not normally think of the human population as something that can be designed. But for the purposes of space colonization, planners will have to take into consideration many factors to populate the habitat with people who will make it function. The number of people will have to be agreed upon. They will have to be members of both sexes, and have different ages and abilities necessary for the benefit of the colony.

Planners looking to the future of space colonization say that they want a combination of families and single people. They also want people of different ethnic backgrounds. Planners assume that the first colony will be populated by people from different industrialized nations. The mixture of these colonists will help determine the form that society and government will take.

Scientists find it relatively easy to plan the construction, architecture, food processing, waste disposal and function of a large space colony. These things can be made to order. But even the wisest planner cannot predict accurately how large numbers of strangers brought together in a new habitat will react.

The people who volunteer for space colonization will have many motives for wanting to live in space, just as all pioneers do. Some will want to take on the challenge of a new and perhaps harsh life. Others will have an idealistic vision about pioneering the future.

Whatever the individual reasons, all of the colonists who live in a space habitat will have to learn how to get along with each other under crowded conditions. They will have to adjust to the fact that there is no escape except for a long and costly trip back to Earth. Planners recognize, however, that all people will not be able to function equally well in space. Some people will feel depressed or out of touch, even though their families and friends are in the same habitat. Therefore, communication with Earth will have to

The "equator" of this 10,000-person space colony is nearly a mile long. There is a small river with shores made of lunar sand. Near the "poles" of the colony, almost-zero gravity would allow colonists to enjoy low-gravity sports. A corridor at the axis would permit floating in zero gravity from one area to another.

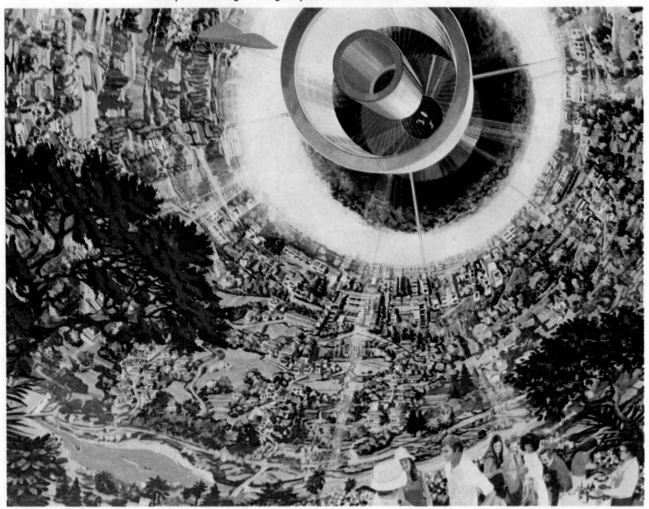

be maintained and there must be ways to return to Earth for people who cannot adjust to their new environment.

Space colonies will have to contain many of the same facilities that are found on Earth. There will have to be homes large enough to live in, shops, offices, schools, hospitals, entertainment centers, recreational facilities, industrial and storage areas and transportation. Scientists believe that the more closely a space station resembles a community on Earth, the easier it will be for people to accept this new way of life.

HOW PEOPLE WILL LIVE

Many of the decisions about space colonies will be based on scientific findings and complicated mathematics. One area that allows planners to use their imaginations is designing how people will live.

The first great adventure for new colonists will be hurtling through space toward the habitat. Just as immigrants

This design for a habitat has a central cylinder 19 miles (32 kilometers) long and 4 miles (6.7 kilometers) in diameter. It would orbit the Earth at the same distance as the moon. Three movable rectangular strip mirrors would create day and night in the habitat.

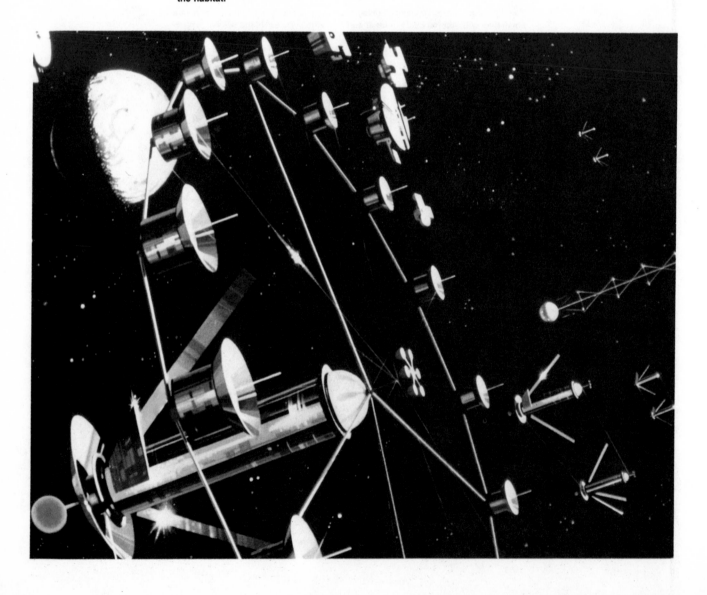

The interior view of the habitat shows how much area within the colony would be devoted to farming. Other agricultural areas could be contained in modules suspended from the habitat. These would be useful for crops requiring highly controlled growing conditions.

from Europe crowded onto the decks of their ships for a glimpse of the Statue of Liberty, colonists aboard a space shuttle will be waiting for their first look at the giant wheel that will be their new home.

As the transport vehicle nears the habitat's docking station, details of the wheel will become visible. Spacecraft manufacturing, ore refining and solar collectors will come into view.

Because the rotation of the hub will be slight, the passengers will disembark into a region with no gravitational pull. As the colonists move through the spokes on an elevator-like conveyance, they will approach the fast-spinning rim of the colony. The sensation of gravity will increase as they get closer to the rim.

The living area of the habitat will be a busy city, but one without skyscrapers or highways. Buildings will be on a human scale and positioned to create the longest sight lines. Architects will use every possible method to create the illusion of greater distances within the habitat.

There will be a central plain around the whole tube and there will be many parks and open plazas. The whole colony will

be bathed in cheerful sunlight, with lush trees and flowers growing everywhere.

Buildings will be terraced up against the habitat's curved walls. The houses will be placed upon one another like layers of a wedding cake. Most residences will have spacious terraces and many windows with attractive views. Mechanical, electrical and plumbing facilities will all be hidden from view in the thick walls of the buildings and under the decks that form the ground.

The houses will be compact and convenient. There will be no wasted space. One of the things the colonists will have to get used to is the absence of wood and plastic in furniture and other items. These products will have to be brought from Earth, while aluminum and ceramics can be produced in the colony from raw materials mined on the moon.

Food for the colonists will be grown aboard the giant rotating wheel. There will be no freeze-dried or dehydrated foods. Instead, the people will eat fresh produce. The habitat's agricultural area will consist of terraced fields, ponds and cascading water. The ponds will hold

Dusk in a giant space colony is depicted in the illustration to the left. The space station is shown in orbit around the Earth, which is creating an eclipse. The illustration below shows the landscape inside the colony. The interior could be made to resemble any part of the Earth.

Twin cylindrical space colonies hovering close to each other would look like this from an approaching spacecraft. The teacup-shaped modules around the colony are agricultural stations. Manufacturing and power stations are at the ends of each colony. Mirrors regulate light to provide seasons and day-night variations.

many varieties of fish. The water will be used to irrigate the crops.

Fields of corn, sorghum, soybeans, rice, alfalfa and vegetables will flourish. Some of these crops will be grown for human consumption while others will be used as fodder for livestock. Planting will be scheduled to provide a continuous supply of fresh produce. Chickens, rabbits and cattle will be raised on one level of these multitiered farms.

A good waste disposal system will be necessary to keep the colony functioning. Sewage, carbon dioxide exhaled by hu-mans and animals and industrial by-products will all be recycled for agricultural purposes. The oxygen and water vapor released by the crops will help sustain the atmosphere inside the space colony.

Space colonists will commute to work on foot or on bicycle. Most jobs will be technical. They will involve sustaining the delicate balance of the space station. Communications, mining and refining materials from space, and manufacturing complicated satellites and spacecraft will be the most important industries. People involved in mining may often travel from

A giant space colony could hold several hundred thousand people. The size of this mammoth habitat is illustrated by the bridge, which is as large as the San Francisco Bay Bridge. City lights are reflected in the mirrors which are used to direct sunlight into the colony's interior.

the habitat to the moon. There will be a lunar base to control activities and provide living quarters for workers.

A DREAM OR A POSSIBILITY?

Putting a space colony for 10,000 people in orbit is not a simple mission. It is really a human proposal to create an entire world. Planners have many ideas of what they think a habitat should be like. But they will not make a guess at when such a costly and complicated mission could be started. They do say, however, that the full timetable for relocating 10,000 people

into a new habitat would take 22 years from start to finish.

The first four years of the project would be devoted to drawing up a plan. From the fifth to the 14th year, a station would be in orbit around the Earth and used as a base for the space colonization project. Up to 400 people would work on this base as it orbited the Earth. At about the 10th year, bases would be built on the moon to assemble the components used to construct the habitat.

The work force on the moon would grow as the lunar base took over many tasks. As the population on the moon increased, the number of people on the Earth-orbiting station would be cut in half. This satellite base would then serve only as a way station.

The shell of the space colony would be built between 12 and 18 years after the project was started. It would be assembled on site from components gathered at the lunar base. Not until early in the 19th year would the first colonists move into the habitat. Planners believe that the population of the colony would increase by 1,000 people a year until it contained 10,000 inhabitants.

It is impossible to estimate how much such a space colony would actually cost. Certainly it would require a great deal of cooperation between government and industry, and planners and colonists. The only safe guess is to say that no colony would be sent off into space until its communications and mining and manufacturing businesses make it pay off. One of the most important roles such a colony would play is in relaying solar energy back to Earth in enormous quantities. Another cost-related benefit would be to use mate-

Scientists' plans for our future in space include more than just space habitats. Project Cyclops is a plan for a series of giant radiotelescope antennae which would be used to detect radio signals from civilizations in parts of the universe as much as 1,000 light years away.

Project Cyclops is a system for the Search for Extraterrestrial Intelligence (SETI). Its physical design is a six-sided arrangement of giant antennae. Each of the 150 antennae is 330 feet (100 meters) in diameter. These high altitude aerial views show how Cyclops would look both on Earth (above) and on the moon (below).

Complete SETI systems, which would probe deep space for evidence of distant civilizations, could eventually be orbited in space. In this illustration an astronaut is shown repairing one of the giant sensors of such a system. The astronaut's spacecraft is shuttle size.

rials from space to replace the Earth's shrinking natural resources.

ON TO LIMITLESS SPACE

The space colonies in science fiction usually travel in deep space, often in galaxies far beyond our own. So far, such voyages are only fiction and fantasy. A functioning space habitat near Earth, however, would be a first step in the quest for further knowledge about distant planets and galaxies. Perhaps these space habitats would be used as launching pads for automated probes that would be sent into the great beyond. The information they gather and transmit back to the space station would prove invaluable to scientists.

Then, if curiosity about mysterious outer space becomes so powerful that we want to send human explorers to chart it, the experience gathered from building and living on space colonies closer to Earth would make such trips possible.

And if and when that happens, frontiers of human knowledge will be pushed far beyond the limits of the immediate future. It will fulfill the wildest fantasies about exploration of the universe.